Ingenious Essays
On
AI And Law

Advanced Series On
Artificial Intelligence (AI)
And Law

Dr. Lance B. Eliot, MBA, PhD

DEDICATION

To my incredible daughter, Lauren, and my incredible son, Michael.

Forest fortuna adiuvat (from the Latin; good fortune favors the brave).

CONTENTS

Note: Visuals are collected together in Appendix B, rather than being interjected into the chapter contents, for ease of reading, enhanced flow, and to see the visuals altogether.

Dr. Lance B. Eliot

ACKNOWLEDGMENTS

I have been the beneficiary of advice and counsel by many friends, colleagues, family, investors, and many others. I want to thank everyone that has aided me throughout my career. I write from the heart and the head, having experienced first-hand what it means to have others around you that support you during the good times and the tough times.

To renowned scholar and colleague, Dr. Warren Bennis, I offer my deepest thanks and appreciation, especially for his calm and insightful wisdom and support.

To billionaire and university trustee, Mark Stevens and his generous efforts toward funding and supporting the Stevens Center for Innovation.

To Peter Drucker, William Wang, Aaron Levie, Peter Kim, Jon Kraft, Cindy Crawford, Jenny Ming, Steve Milligan, Chis Underwood, Frank Gehry, Buzz Aldrin, Steve Forbes, Bill Thompson, Dave Dillon, Alan Fuerstman, Larry Ellison, Jim Sinegal, John Sperling, Mark Stevenson, Anand Nallathambi, Thomas Barrack, Jr., and many other innovators and leaders that I have met and gained mightily from doing so.

Thanks to Ed Trainor, Kevin Anderson, James Hickey, Wendell Jones, Ken Harris, DuWayne Peterson, Mike Brown, Jim Thornton, Abhi Beniwal, Al Biland, John Nomura, Eliot Weinman, John Desmond, and many others for their unwavering support during my career.

Thanks goes to the Stanford University CodeX Center for Legal Informatics and the Stanford University Computer Science department for their generous support, and for the insightful and inspirational discussions and feedback from my many fellow colleagues there.

And most of all thanks as always to Lauren and Michael, for their ongoing support and for having seen me writing and heard much of this material during the many months involved in writing it. To their patience and willingness to listen.

Dr. Lance B. Eliot

CHAPTER 1

INTRODUCTION TO
AI AND LAW

This book provides a series of ingenious essays encompassing the burgeoning field of AI and the law.

These essays are ostensibly standalone and do not require any prior familiarity with the AI and law topic. You are welcome to read the essays in whichever order you might prefer. The essays have been numbered and sequenced as chapters for ease of referring to the discussions and not due to any need to read one before another.

The essays provide a helpful overview and entry point into the field of AI and law. You will find the essays relatively easy to read and eschew arcane techno-terminology, aiming to layout the vital aspects in clear language and seeking to be readily grasped. The chosen topics entail the latest and hottest trends in the AI and law arena.

For those of you that are potentially interested in knowing more about AI and the law in a deeper way, you might consider my other books on this subject:

- *"AI and Legal Reasoning Essentials"* by Dr. Lance Eliot

- *"Artificial Intelligence and LegalTech Essentials"* by Dr. Lance Eliot

- *"Decisive Essays on AI and Law"* by Dr. Lance Eliot

- *"Incisive Research on AI and Law"* by Dr. Lance Eliot

The first two books are more akin to textbook-style orientations to the AI and the law field.

The other two books are a further collection of my essays and the latter book contains my in-depth research papers (oriented toward legal and AI scholars). The books are available on Amazon and at major bookseller sites.

One of the most frequent questions that I get asked during my webinars, seminars, and university courses about AI and the law consists of what the phrase "AI and the law" actually refers to.

That's a fair question and deserves a useful answer. In a moment, I will borrow from my other books to provide an explanation about the meaning of "AI and the law" and then dovetail into a brief indication about each of the essays contained in this collection.

Per the essays, you'll end up seeing that there is a great deal of enthusiastic spirit for AI and the law, and likewise a sizable dollop of angst and trepidation about the intertwining of the two. In my view, whether you love it or hate it, there is no stopping the steamroller moving ahead that is going to infuse AI together with the law.

I would urge that any lawyer worth their salt ought to be learning about AI and the law. This will assuredly be especially important for those that are just now starting their legal careers, which I mention because the odds are that the convergence of AI and the law will have an especially pronounced effect throughout your lifelong legal efforts.

For those of you that might be going a more so academic route in the legal realm, rather than being a practitioner of the law per se, the beauty of AI and the law is that there is ample room for new research and a grand opportunity to make a demonstrative mark on the field. There are numerous open questions and plenty of challenges that provide abundant possibility for making a decided mark on this still nascent field of study.

Despite the fact that the field of AI and the law has been studied for many years, dating back to the beginning of the AI field itself, please be aware that we have only scratched the surface on this interweaving. Anyone with a desire to push the boundaries of these two realms will readily find plenty of rampways to do so.

If you are curious about the possible research avenues to pursue, make sure to take a look at my book on *AI and Legal Reasoning Essentials* since it provides a solid foundation on the research to-date and postulates what might be coming down the pike in future research activities, and then consider my book on *Incisive Research on AI and Law.* I bid you welcome to the field and wish you the best of luck in your endeavors.

I next provide a brief introduction to the field of AI and law, which echoes my thoughts as variously expressed in my other books and my various articles and postings.

AI And Law

In my viewpoint, Artificial Intelligence (AI) and the field of law are synergistic partners. The intertwining of AI and Law can generally be categorized into two major approaches:

- **AI as applied to Law**
- **Law as applied to AI**

Let us consider each of those two approaches.

AI As Applied To Law

AI as applied to law consists of trying to utilize AI technologies and AI techniques for the embodiment of law, potentially being able to perform legal tasks and undertake legal reasoning associated with the practice of law. Those scholars, experts, and practitioners that have this focus are using AI to aid or integrate artificial intelligence into how humans practice law, either augmenting lawyers and other legal professionals or possibly replacing them in the performance of various legal tasks.

Crafting such AI is especially hard to accomplish, problematic in many ways, and there have been and continue to emerge a myriad of attempts to achieve this difficult goal or aspiration.

The rise of LegalTech and LawTech, which is modern digital technology used to support and enable lawyers, law offices, and the like throughout the practice of law are gradually and inexorably being bolstered by the addition of AI capabilities.

There are many indications already of this trend rapidly expanding in the existing and growing LegalTech and LawTech marketplace. Notably, the potent AI and LegalTech/LawTech combination has been drawing the rapt attention of Venture Capitalists (VCs). According to figures by the National Venture Capital Association (NVCA), the last several years have witnessed VC's making key investments of over one billion dollars towards law-related tech startups, many of which have some form of an AI capability involved.

Most of the AI developed so far for LegalTech and LawTech is only able to assist lawyers and legal professions in rather modest and simplistic ways. For example, AI might speed-up the search for documents during e-discovery or might enhance the preparation of a contract by identifying pertinent contractual language from a corpus of prior contracts.

Where the field of applying AI to law is seeking to head involves having AI that can perform legal minded tasks that human lawyers and other legal professionals perform. In essence, creating AI systems that can undertake legal reasoning. This is commonly referred to as AI for Legal Reasoning (AILR).

In a sense, legal reasoning goes to the core of performing legal tasks and is considered the ultimate pinnacle as it were for the efforts to try and apply AI to law. It is undoubtedly one of the most exciting areas of the AI-applied-to-law arena and one that holds both tremendous promise and perhaps some angst and possible somber qualms.

Law As Applied To AI

The other major approach that combines AI and law focuses on the law as applied AI. This is an equally crucial perspective on the AI and law topic.

Sometimes this is also referred to as the **Governance of AI**, though there are those that believe that to be a somewhat narrower perspective on the topic. In any case, the focus is primarily on the governance of AI and how our laws might need to be revised, updated, or revamped in light of AI systems.

You likely already know that AI is experiencing quite a resurgence and has become a key focus of the tech field, along with gaining attention throughout society. AI is being rapidly infused into a wide variety of industries and domain specialties, including AI in the financial sector, AI in the medical domain, and so on.

This rapid pace of AI adoption has opened the eyes of society about the benefits of AI but also has gradually brought to the forefront many of the costs or negative aspects that AI can bring forth. Some assert that our existing laws are insufficient to cope with the advances that AI is producing. Thus, the need to closely examine our existing laws and possibly revamp them for an era and future of ubiquitous AI.

Expected Impacts

Let's consider how AI and the law can impact those in the AI field, and also contemplate how it can impact those in the field of law.

If you are an AI specialist, you should certainly be interested in the AI and law topic, either due to the possibilities of advancing AI by discovering how to leverage AI into the legal domain or due to the potential of how existing and future laws are going to impact the exploration and fielding of AI systems.

If you are a lawyer or legal specialist, you ought to be interested in the AI and law topic too, for the same reasons as the AI specialist, though perhaps with some added stake in the game.

What is the added stake?

If AI can ultimately become advanced enough to practice law, there is concern by some that it could potentially replace the need for human lawyers and other human legal-related law practitioners.

Some liken this to the famous and telling remark about commitment as exhibited via a chicken and a pig. A chicken and a pig are walking along and discussing what they might do together, and the chicken offers that perhaps they ought to open a restaurant that serves ham-n-eggs. Upon a moment of reflection, the pig speaks up and says that if they did so, the chicken would only be involved (making the eggs), while the pig would end-up being fully committed (being the bacon).

In that sense, AI specialists in this topic are involved, while legal specialists and lawyers are committed. Meanwhile, for those of you squarely in the field of law, lest you think that AI specialists are to be spared the same fate of being overtaken by AI, you will be perhaps surprised to know that there are efforts underway to craft AI that makes AI, such as in the field of Machine Learning (ML), a specialty known as AutoML, which could potentially put human developers of AI out of a job. What is good for the goose is good for the gander. Or, it might be that what is bad for the goose is equally bad for the gander.

About These Essays

Now that you've gotten an initial synopsis regarding the topic of AI and law, let's take a moment to briefly take a look at the essays assembled for this decisive collection.

Chapter 1 – Introduction To AI And Law

Key briefing points about this chapter:

- This book is a collection of crucial essays about AI and the law

- The essays are provided as numbered chapters (the sequence is not essential)

- AI and the law consist of two key facets

- One facet is AI as applied to the law (a mainstay of this collection)

- The other facet is applying the law to AI (i.e., governance of AI)

Chapter 2 - AI & Law: Wittgenstein Rules Paradox

Key briefing points about this chapter:

- One of life's considered blind spots is not knowing what you don't know

- In the case of any methods or approaches based on rules, the "don't know" possibility exists

- Ludwig Wittgenstein famously identified this rules-oriented paradox and a warning thereof

- There is an apparent impact on human attorneys and their practice of the law

- Likewise is an apparent impact on AI-based legal reasoning systems and the future therein

Chapter 3 - AI & Law: Deskilling of Human Lawyers

Key briefing points about this chapter:

- Attorneys are expected to provide topnotch legal acumen and serve their clients sufficiently

- Some are worried that the emergence of AI in the law will cause a deskilling of lawyers

- Attorneys will be able to rely upon AI-based legal reasoning systems for legal advisement

- The crutch of using AI could lead to a deskilling of human lawyers

- One viewpoint is that this is a futuristic concern, others see it as close-in and discomforting

Chapter 4 - **AI & Law: Bar Exam Interactive Testing**

Key briefing points about this chapter:

- The bar exam is a crucial barrier-to-entry for budding attorneys
- It is presumed that the bar exam aids in ensuring that lawyers are properly vetted for practice
- Advances in technology and pervasive of tech will enable online bar exams and interactivity
- One possibility consists of having an AI-enabled interrogator during a bar exam taking
- There is a belief that the AI could further the aim of ensuring attorneys are ready to go

Chapter 5 - **AI & Law: AI-Based Adjudication Dispassionate**

Key briefing points about this chapter:

- Tremendous effort has gone into the exploration of how judges think
- A longstanding assertion is that judges should set aside all emotion and sentimentality
- Meanwhile, lately, there has been criticism that AI-based legal systems will lack emotion
- This begs the question of whether AI is better or worse off as a dispassionate judge
- Though the added twist is that AI can indeed be infused with emotion if we so desire

Chapter 6 - AI & Law: BigLaw

Key briefing points about this chapter:

- Law firms of any notable size are especially tricky to manage and ably adjust to market shifts

- BigLaw is viewed as likely to have internal squabbles over the advent of AI-based legal services

- Some law firms will quickly embrace AI, others will ignore or deflect AI emerging changes

- One prediction is that BigLaw will inexorably have to adapt to and utilize AI or suffer woes

- Thus expect to see BigLaw ultimately grasp onto and embody AI-based legal services

Chapter 7 - AI & Law: Canons of Contradiction

Key briefing points about this chapter:

- Attorneys generally seek to craft the strongest possible argument favoring their side of a case

- The human foible of anchoring to your own posture can undermine the strength of an argument

- Best to always keep in mind the legendary *canons of construction* by legal scholar Llewellyn

- Another perspective is to consider these as mindful *canons of contradiction*

- These canons raise interesting prospects and potential difficulties for AI-enabled legal reasoning

Chapter 8 - AI & Law: Paperclip Maximizer Qualms

Key briefing points about this chapter:

- Paperclips have more importance than might be apparent to the ordinary eye

- Turns out that a parable involving paperclips has been an AI "hot topic" for many years

- Suppose an AI system went overboard and made paperclips obediently but to our detriment

- This same unintentional adverse consequence could befall the use of AI in the law

- Knowing about the paperclip predicament can help guide AI adoption in the legal field

Chapter 9 – AI & Law: Questions of Effective AI Counsel

Key briefing points about this chapter:

- The Sixth Amendment ensures that criminal defendants will have the assistance of legal counsel

- An unstated but implied facet is that such legal counsel will perform in an effective manner

- *Strickland v. Washington* ruling of the Supreme Court laid out the effectiveness parameters

- Some criticize though that the two-parts effectiveness guidelines are overly open-ended

- Effectiveness will remain a vital consideration even in an era of AI-based legal reasoning

Chapter 10 - AI & Law: Multijurisdictional Lawyering

Key briefing points about this chapter:

- There are existing state-by-state admissions requirements for attorneys wishing to switch states

- Some assert that the matter is byzantine, unorderly, unnecessary, and a legal morass

- Multijurisdictional arguments are in camps: Open borders, strict borders, permeable borders

- Consider that eventually and some believe inevitably there will be AI-based legal reasoning

- AI-based legal reasoning will be incrementally devised and has multijurisdictional ramifications

Chapter 11 - AI & Law: Digital Twin of the Constitution

Key briefing points about this chapter:

- Many assert that the United States Constitution is a living document

- Acrimonious debates occur over what the meaning of this "living" document ought to be

- Numerous camps have evolved about how to properly interpret the Constitution

- In modern times there are digital twins being developed for all kinds of entities

- It is useful to consider crafting an AI-based digital twin of the Constitution

Chapter 12 - AI & Law: Antitrust and AI (AAI)

Key briefing points about this chapter:

- Antitrust law has once again been brought to the forefront of society
- A recent spate of antitrust lawsuits against tech firms catches the eye and worldwide attention
- We need to be cautious in overstepping our instant assumption that antitrust has occurred
- To aid in the antitrust vigilance proposition we can adopt the use of AI for antitrust endeavors
- Via the use of AI-based antitrust diligence systems, the vigilance can be notably enhanced

Chapter 13 – AI & Law: AI Arbitrator Impartiality Issues

Key briefing points about this chapter:

- Arbitration consists of one or more arbitrators and the associated parties to the case
- A party might accuse an arbitrator of having biases that impacted impartiality
- Disclosure pre-case is intended to aid in avoiding selecting a potentially biased arbitrator
- Futurists of the law are anticipating that AI will have a notable role in arbitrations
- Turns out it is a commonly accepted false assumption that the AI will be bereft of biases

Chapter 14 – AI & Law: Think Fast and Think Slow

Key briefing points about this chapter:

- A popular metacognition model is that humans have a twofold approach to how our minds work

- One portion of our minds thinks fast, making snap decisions, called *System 1* (M-consciousness)

- The other portion thinks slow, analytically so, and is known as *System 2* (I-consciousness)

- This viewpoint about the mind can be applied to lawyers and performing legal reasoning

- AI has likewise the sub-symbolics and the symbolics camps

Chapter 15 - AI & Law: Legal Personhood

Key briefing points about this chapter:

- One means of applying the law to AI consists of considering how to best legally govern AI

- There are ongoing debates about whether AI should or should not have legal personhood

- Sometimes an argument is aided by looking at extremes

- An extreme viewpoint of today's AI is the notion of a future kind of AI known as spontaneous

- Discussion of a spontaneous form of AI gives new potential insights for the governance of AI

Chapter 16 – AI & Law: Lower Courts and AI Judges

Key briefing points about this chapter:

- There is much debate about the possibility of AI serving as judges in our courts

- Some argue it should never be permitted, others say it will be inevitable and unstoppable

- One argument being made is that perhaps AI judges would be solely used in the lower courts

- The logic for use at the lower courts includes scalability and consistency

- Countering points are that this drains humanity from the lower courts and is a slippery slope

Chapter 17 - AI & Law: Representational Conflicts

Key briefing points about this chapter:

- Lawyers are to avoid conflicts of interest in the lawyer-client relationship

- It is hard to imagine one attorney vigorously representing two opposing clients

- The future of the law includes the infusion of AI-based legal reasoning systems

- We will ultimately have AI that can be the lawyer in the lawyer-client relationship

- Consider whether there are potential conflicts of interest by that AI representation

Chapter 18 - AI & Law: Overzealous Lawyering

Key briefing points about this chapter:

- Clients expect their attorney to be a vigorous and spirited legal representative

- This is also a requirement for the essence of our adversarial structure of justice

- But sometimes a lawyer goes overboard and stretches into being overzealous

- Overzealousness is a debatable threshold, nonetheless, sanctions can be applied

- In a future with AI-based attorneys, overzealousness (surprisingly) will still be at issue

Chapter 19 - AI & Law: Hybrid Neuro-Symbolic AI

Key briefing points about this chapter:

- The use of Machine Learning (ML) continues to gain ground, including in the legal profession

- Many wonder whether the future of AI is entirely pegged to further advances solely in ML

- Some predict ML will hit a proverbial wall, and that rules-based approaches will be reborn

- These two camps (often warring) are known as the sub-symbolic and the symbolics

- A hybrid AI also referred to as neuro-symbolic, might be the way forward, for the law too

Chapter 20 - **AI & Law: Law Schools**

Key briefing points about this chapter:

- Few law schools offer a formal course on the topic of AI and the law

- Sometimes the AI and law topic haphazardly comes up during regular law classes

- There are bona fide reasons for adopting such classes and for opting to not do so

- The key arguments made on the pro and con side of this coin are equally compelling

- It would seem inevitable that someday this course will officially be at most law schools

Chapter 21 - **AI & Law: Chicken Or The Egg**

Key briefing points about this chapter:

- Which came first, the chicken or the egg?

- It seems that a compelling case can be made for either side, though argumentatively so

- An interesting likening to the advent of AI and the law raises akin infinite regress issues

- Ought the law be pointing fingers at the human that launched the AI or the AI itself

- A legal scholar has coined this the homunculus fallacy and warns to avoid sleight of hand

Chapter 22 – AI & Law: Legal Jargon

Key briefing points about this chapter:

- Legalese or legal jargon is oftentimes criticized by both non-lawyers and lawyers alike

- There is a case to be made for the basis of having legal language and specialized lingo

- Nonetheless, there is concern about the use of so-called lawyering "weasel words"

- Some seem to believe or hope that the adoption of AI in the law will obviate such lingo

- It is argued herein that this is a false assumption and quite unlikely an outcome of AI use

Chapter 23 - AI & Law: Legal Chess Playing

Key briefing points about this chapter:

- Some liken the practice of law to the playing of chess

- Lawyers need to conceive of their legal moves and countermoves related to opposing counsel

- AI chess-playing systems have gotten quite good and there are lessons to be learned therein

- It is handy to consider the state-space complexity in the construct of legal argumentation

- Predictions are that the use of AI legal reasoning will ultimately be integral to legal arguments

Chapter 24 - AI & Law: Setting The Bar On Proficiency

Key briefing points about this chapter:

- Consider the difficulties of trying to rate and compare new movies
- This can be done by contrasting with ones that same year, or all-time, or versus perfection
- Shifting gears, AI-based legal reasoning systems will gradually be introduced and utilized
- The proficiency of such AI systems to practice law will certainly come into question
- This raises the matter of rating, AI versus AI, or AI versus human lawyering, or perfection

Chapter 25 - AI & Law: Repeatedly Trying Is Sane

Key briefing points about this article:

- Popular these days is that repeatedly doing something is insane if expecting a differing result
- Claimed as attributable to Einstein, there is no indication he said this
- Furthermore, as an alleged truism, it is misleading and faulty
- This comes up since it is being used by skeptics that doubt the efficacy of AI in the law
- They fail to realize that there are under-the-hood differences, thus premature exhortations

More About This Book

For anyone opting to use this book in a class or course that pertains to these topics, note that Appendix A contains suggestions about how to use the book in a classroom setting.

Furthermore, Appendix B contains a set of slides that depict many of the salient points made throughout the book.

In some of my prior books, I've interspersed the slides into the chapter contents, but feedback by readers has generally been that readers prefer to not have the textual flow become disrupted by the slides, and instead prefer to have the supplemental material assembled altogether into an appendix.

To make sure that you are aware of those added materials, you'll notice that the ending of each chapter provides a quick reminder about the visual depictions that are available in Appendix B.

And so, with this overall orientation to the nature and structure of this book in mind, please proceed to read the essays and learn about the field of AI and law. I'm truly hoping that you'll find the essays mentally engaging and stimulative to the nature of how the law is being practiced and what the future of the law might become.

Note: *For supplemental materials depicting the aspects discussed in this chapter, refer to Appendix B, which contains various augmented diagrams, charts, and additional related facets of relevance.*

CHAPTER 2

AI & LAW: WITTGENSTEIN RULES PARADOX

Key briefing points about this essay:

- One of life's considered blind spots is not knowing what you don't know

- In the case of any methods or approaches based on rules, the "don't know" possibility exists

- Ludwig Wittgenstein famously identified this rules-oriented paradox and a warning thereof

- There is an apparent impact on human attorneys and their practice of the law

- Likewise is an apparent impact on AI-based legal reasoning systems and the future therein

Introduction

What do you know and when did you come to realize that you know it?

Are there things you don't know, which you know that you don't know? And, do you think there may be things you don't know, for which you don't know that you don't know them?

Some assert that the things you don't know that you don't know are the most insidious and most likely to undermine your wellbeing. This popular maxim seems indubitably to make a lot of sense. One state of mind is the act of not knowing something. Another state of mind is at least having the awareness or acknowledgment that you do not know the something that you do not know. Worse of all would seem to not only be absent of knowing a something but on top of that to not even realize that you don't know it. All in all, a somewhat topsy-turvy road, perhaps, yet there is some axiomatic and abundant soundness to these notions.

Since we are venturing into a realm of ostensibly deep thoughts, it might be interesting to take a step further into what some refer to as the physics of law.

In short, some espouse the idea that the law is amenable to a form of physics or the rigors that we believe coincides with our understanding of physics and the innate and apparently immutable principles of nature. Perhaps all the trappings of law are really just another variant of physics, presently cloaked from obvious discovery, and our existing ad hoc treatment of the law is due to not having uncovered those inherent and still hidden underlying truths and precepts.

Per this kind of perspective, the law is ostensibly a science that up until now has borne the attention of an art. Were we to shift our viewpoint and recast the artistry of law into the science of law, potentially there would be a much stronger semblance of rigor in the nature of law and how we practice law.

You might refer to this in another way, namely, we seemingly don't know that we don't know that the law is actually a collective of ironclad rules and logic befitting the manner by which we can also depict and comprehend the structure of the universe and all the matter within it.

Mind blown.

Continuing this train of thought, consider a logic-based riddle of sorts that has become known as the Wittgenstein rules paradox and pertains substantively to the law, along with stoking keen and essential insights for the attempts at achieving the application of Artificial Intelligence (AI) to the law.

Grasping The Rule Of Wittgenstein

Ludwig Wittgenstein in 1953 sowed quite a seed of doubt about the use of rules, in general, which therefore would presumably also apply to the potential use and application of legal rules. Here is what he said: "This was our paradox: no course of action could be determined by a rule, because any course of action can be made out to accord with the rule" (per his book entitled *Philosophical Investigations*).

Wittgenstein's commentary is at first glance rather mystifying. Let's delve briefly into the mystery and showcase the demonstrative power of what he was insightfully pointing out.

Suppose I ask you to tell me what the arithmetic answer to this is:

- What is 10 + 23?

Obviously, your answer is 33.

Suppose I ask you what the arithmetic answer to this is:

- What is 42 + 16?

Your answer is 58.

And so on, we can continue like this nearly endlessly, presumably. Now, here's the twist.

Answer this arithmetic question:

- What is 60 + 12?

I assume your answer is 72.

But suppose I told you that was wrong, and that the correct answer is 5.

You would certainly be skeptical that the answer is 5.

Turns out, I offer an explanation for my answer that somewhat shocks your sensibilities about the world, which is as follows: Unbeknownst to you, all along there is has been a rule that we'll give the name of "quus" (any moniker will do), and this rule states:

- x **quus** y
- **quus** indicates: $x + y$ **for** x, y < 57
- **quus** also indicates: **5 for** x >= 57 **or** y >= 57

Thus, when you were asked to add together 60 + 12, this meant that x was 60 and y was 12, and that since x is the value of 60, which is greater than 57, the final result to be indicated is the number 5. Meanwhile, the prior question about adding together 42 + 16 would be the answer 58 via the rules of quus, and likewise, the answer to 10 + 23 would be the number 33, both instances of which comported with your prior understanding of the arithmetic function of addition, yet were insufficient examples to give rise to surfacing the role of the quus function or rule.

Wittgenstein's point was that though you might assume that the arithmetic function of addition is one type of function or rule, it might be something else, such as it might contain the (made-up) quus function or rules too (or, any other such function, functions, rule, or rules). In fact, there could be any number of such quus-like functions that are hidden or buried within any system of rules, and you might not know it.

Speaking of not knowing, imagine that I had kept asking you to add numbers together and never reached any that were above the x and y of being at least 57. Presumably, you would unknowingly believe that the arithmetic function was always and inarguably the conventional x + y, simply due to never encountering the special case of x or y being at least 57.

How does that impact legal reasoning?

You might believe that you've figured out some set of legal rules that encompass legal reasoning and perhaps as you utilize them in the daily course of your practice of law, they seem to work quite well. But it is conceivable that you've failed to include in your set some hidden or unrealized legal rules or functions akin to the quus lesson.

There might not just be one quus, there might be an infinite number of such as-yet-unknown legal rules.

Another way to look at it is that any legal rule that you might come up with, and which might seem satisfying, could very well not be the "right" rule and only something that seems for the moment to be the appropriate rule. Then, upon the (perhaps) happenstance discovery of a new rule, like quus, the set might be turned on its head, doing so under the belated realization that all along the "wrong" rules were being used (the notion of "wrong" is somewhat ambiguous since the rules could have been correct and yet incomplete, or alternatively they could be entirely incorrect).

Ramifications For AI Legal Reasoning Too

So, when trying to devise rules for legal reasoning, we could either decide that it is useless to try and essentially give up the pursuit, conceding that the Wittgenstein rules paradox has ensnared us, or we could proceed but need to always keep at the forefront of our thinking that the rules paradox is a bona fide and useful warning about what we have achieved.

Stripping away some of the complexity of this somewhat esoteric rules paradox, any seasoned lawyer has likely witnessed these quus-like phenomena among newbie attorneys or potentially amidst budding law students. Those eager legal beagles might have latched onto some set of legal rules and believe they have fully accounted for all the underlying precepts needed to resolve a case.

There is nothing more delightful for a savvy lawyer, it would seem, but to burst the naïve bubble of those apprentices than to showcase an additional rule that with a flourish dashes their limited rule set and opens wide a completely different path or a cornucopia of challenges.

That being said, even the best of lawyers and having the brightest of minds are still subject to the same Wittgenstein rules paradox. It would seem the height of egotism to presume that one already knew all the possible rules and legal reasoning and therefore had no need to inquire any further. Research of experienced lawyers tends to suggest that they are always wary that there is a legal rule still unsurfaced and that could either be the winning move for a pressing case or might gut their argument and push them toward legal defeat.

All of this weighs heavily on the advent of AI in the law.

For those devising AI-based legal reasoning systems, there is the haunting possibility that the Wittgenstein rules paradox will underly their efforts. Whenever crafting the zillions of legal rules needed to have an AI-powered legal reasoner, there is that chance that there are omitted rules, potentially overarching and overriding rules, thus the AI is bereft of the needed basis for appropriately being considered a valid practitioner of the law.

Of course, a counterargument exists that if humans are likewise subject to the same failing, do we unreasonably expect that the AI legal reasoning systems should necessarily not also be so confounded. Perhaps there is no choice but to accept the paradoxical possibility in both the case of human attorneys and those AI-based legal reasoning systems.

The fervent hope would be to keep a wary eye open and undertake diligent and ongoing monitoring, seeking to as early as possible ascertain that such a predicament exists and then make needed changes accordingly.

Conclusion

Prudence dictates that being on the watch for that which we don't know, staying on top of knowing that we don't know, provides some solace toward the ever-present existence of not knowing what we don't know..

Note: *For supplemental materials depicting the aspects discussed in this chapter, refer to Appendix B, which contains various augmented diagrams, charts, and additional related facets of relevance*

CHAPTER 3
AI & LAW:
DESKILLING OF
HUMAN LAWYERS

Key briefing points about this essay:

- Attorneys are expected to provide topnotch legal acumen and serve their clients sufficiently

- Some are worried that the emergence of AI in the law will cause a deskilling of lawyers

- Attorneys will be able to rely upon AI-based legal reasoning systems for legal advisement

- The crutch of using AI could lead to a deskilling of human lawyers

- One viewpoint is that this is a futuristic concern, others see it as close-in and discomforting

Introduction

Attorneys are expected to always be providing the best possible legal advice and topnotch legal acumen, doing so not simply due to some altruistic quest but to equally ensure they are aiding their clients sufficiently and properly, plus warranting that they are abiding by the esteemed code-of-conduct required of licensed practitioners of the law.

Is it realistic to always be at the top of your game? You might remember that in the movie *Top Gun* (spoiler alert), Tom Cruise loses his edge and no longer seems to feel the need, the need for speed, in terms of being at the top of his game. Perhaps lawyers can likewise have their bad days, possibly bad weeks or months, and fall off their edge, as it were.

Some are asserting that assuredly this will be the case, coming about due to the advent of Artificial Intelligence (AI) and the law.

This gloomy future for human attorneys is based on the presumption that the use of AI will increasingly take on the mental mechanizations involved in legal reasoning and be able to perform legal tasks as ably as human lawyers, perhaps even better so.

The most extreme version entails the wholescale and utter replacement of human lawyers altogether.

Once AI has reached the pinnacle state of being able to fully and autonomously perform AI Legal Reasoning (AILR), the days of human attorneys being needed are ruefully numbered. AI would presumably be available 24x7 to dispense bona fide legal advice and be had at the touch of one's fingertips on a computer keyboard or by speaking to an Alex or Siri equivalent. No hassle to find or access true legal advice.

Perhaps the cost too would be less than that of human barristers.

Some emphasize an era of frictionless online access to always-on legal advice at pennies on the dollar versus the more arduous access to find and interact with human attorneys, along with no longer having to deal with the vagaries of human foibles and everyday annoyances of human interaction (ouch, that's a piercing and insolent attack, for sure).

AI-Based Legal Reasoners Still Afar

Before you give up your law degree and legal standing, please know that this kind of AI containing legal expertise of a sentient capacity is a long way from where things stand today.

There is a high hurdle involved in replicating the cognitive capacities of legal reasoning into a computer-based system and no silver bullet or magic wand has appeared on the horizon to do so. Those that point to AI that can play chess at mastery levels or that can potentially steer a self-driving car are apt to forewarn that AI is on the heels of crashing down into the ranks of attorneys.

Make no mistake, there is a vast and miles deep chasm between AI automation achieving those "easier" types of AI applications, thus it is assuredly misleading and mistaken to lump them together as though they are roughly the same. The indeterminate semantics inherent in legal reasoning and the linguistic cognitive complexities in performing legal advisory services are more challenging and less apt to being conquered via today's variant of AI (which, as a precautionary note, there might be later advances in AI that crack that code and therefore it is best to not become complacent or lulled into a sense of human superiority merely by how contemporary AI functions).

Let's then momentarily agree that the doomsday predictions of AI having fully autonomous legal reasoning is a moonshot (or maybe akin to living on Mars) and not worthy of staying awake right now worrying about it.

Do not though breathe an excessive sigh of relief since the woods still cast predatory apprehensions.

Instead of getting caught up in the vision of a world in which AI is fully autonomous and can perform entirely fluent legal reasoning, consider what it might mean as the earth gradually rotates in that direction. Some suggest that as more and more e-Discovery tools are embellished via AI, and as contract generation tools become boosted by AI-enablement, and so on, there will be a gradual and at times imperceptible deskilling of human lawyers.

Yes, the qualm is that human lawyers will allow their lawyering skills to decay and diminish, becoming reliant on advanced LegalTech that will do much of the heavy legal lifting for them.

An indirect and presumably adverse consequence of adopting AI-augmented legal tools will be that the human attorneys essentially practice less and less law per se, at least in terms of using their own minds. Ironically, attorneys might end-up tackling more legal cases at faster speeds and impressively up their productivity, but meanwhile, they are silently and (perhaps unknowingly) deskilling themselves.

Shift gears and ponder the rancorous debates about what is potentially happening to the youth of our society due to the ubiquitous availability of Google search or equivalent on-line search options. It is argued that kids no longer need to memorize facts and concepts, being armed instead of having access to the Internet. Why bother to learn something when you know it is readily retrievable online? Some alarmingly argue that contemporary children are going to become future adults that have hollow minds, barren of the stuff that we were forced to learn. This upcoming generation eschews the prior obsession with in-your-brain knowledge, labeling it as exceedingly superfluous since an online database or system houses whatever they might need to know.

Dare we ask or suggest, perhaps lawyers will go the same route?

Note that this will not happen overnight. There isn't a sudden burst of bright light that warns us of the deskilling amidst lawyers. It is instead a slow death of a thousand gradual cuts. Inch by inch, foot by foot, as AI is infused into LegalTech, and as human lawyers use that LegalTech, the human legal mind will weaken and no longer feel the need all told, as in the need for being on top of the law and nor at the top of their legal game.

Don't remember or know important legal cases and precedents? No big deal, just look it up. Aren't sure what aspects of the law pertain to a new case you've opted to take on. Easy peasy, ask the AI what to do and, then (possibly mindlessly) follow those instructions. Need a double-check to make sure your legal briefs are sound? Don't waste time asking a fellow partner, instead have the AI perform a legal review for you.

Proverbial AI Trojan Horse

AI-powered LegalTech becomes a Trojan horse.

In the door of the law offices it comes, while at the same time out the door goes the legal mental prowess of the firm's attorneys and legal staff. AI is the ultimate deskilling machine, but it doesn't have any stern warning labels to proffer the necessary precautions and awareness thereof.

If all of that is the lawyer deskilling slippery slope, one supposes that you could simply and unflinchingly refuse to make use of AI-enabled LegalTech. Put down your foot and declare that no AI will be permitted anywhere that your legal team exists. Not in the office, and not in the courtroom. Not in a box, and not with a fox, as Dr. Seuss might have clued us earlier in life.

Well, sorry to say, for those Luddites that wish to toss monkey wrenches into the machinery, it is a head-in-the-sand viewpoint and will only mean that you and your associates will get run over by those that do embrace the AI wares. To be clear, LegalTech is embracing AI and will continue relentlessly to do so. Trying to turn back the clock won't stop and nor even dent the march toward AI-based legal reasoning capabilities.

Before a semblance of despair overtakes your legal beagle talents, please do not toss in the towel on this matter.

A strong counterargument to the deskilling narrative is that the augmenting of human lawyering with AI-enabled tools will be more akin to arming attorneys with word processing and spreadsheets, namely boosting their legal wrangling acumen. Human attorneys will be able to focus their attention on the tougher acts of doing earnest probing and mental chess playing entailing complex legal analyses, leaving the mundane law-related activities to the AI.

The analogy often given is that the AI-powered LegalTech is akin to giving someone a souped-up backhoe or some likened tool. The human no longer does the backbreaking work and instead can concentrate on grander mental facets such as planning what needs to be done and devising more extensive efforts accordingly.

It would seem misguided to argue that the use of legal online databases has undermined legal mental acuity. The same goes for all the other variants of LegalTech that presently exists.

In fact, the argument could be made that these computer-based tools have allowed legal minds to soar further than ever, having ready access to larger stores of legal information and relieving attorneys of getting bogged down in trivia or minutia.

In that sense, perhaps AI-enabled LegalTech will upskill human lawyers rather than deskill them.

Not wishing to end this discussion on a somber note, but some concede the upskilling, and yet also forewarn that it once again is a trap.

There will be a cat and mouse gambit of the human attorneys getting better at the law, meanwhile, the AI is getting better too. Eventually, the AI will get so good that the human attorneys will no longer be needed. The human lawyers inadvertently aided the advancement of the very thing that in the end replaced them.

Conclusion

Nothing stings more than working yourself out of a job and a career.

Fortunately, that's a worry for a far-future generation of human lawyers, so you can proceed without hesitation, and maybe hope that the promise of autonomous AI legal reasoning will either never happen or that humans by then will have across-the-board advanced such that we will no longer be working in any kind of occupation or labor, shifting instead to a life of pure leisure while the AI does all real-world work for us.

Do not give up your day job in the meantime.

Note: *For supplemental materials depicting the aspects discussed in this chapter, refer to Appendix B, which contains various augmented diagrams, charts, and additional related facets of relevance.*

CHAPTER 4
AI & LAW:
BAR EXAM
INTERACTIVE TESTING

Key briefing points about this essay:

- The bar exam is a crucial barrier-to-entry for budding attorneys

- It is presumed that the bar exam aids in ensuring that lawyers are properly vetted for practice

- Advances in technology and pervasive of tech will enable online bar exams and interactivity

- One possibility consists of having an AI-enabled interrogator during a bar exam taking

- There is a belief that the AI could further the aim of ensuring attorneys are ready to go

Introduction

The dreaded bar exam.

Budding attorneys have nightmares about taking the test. Careers are on the line. Furthermore, everyone you know will feel let down if you don't pass.

All those that have supported you in the years-long quest to become a lawyer will wonder what has happened and how you went astray. Suppose you aren't able to pass the bar exam, ever, what will become of you?

For those that already succeeded at the bar exam, after a while the prior burdensome weight of taking the test seems to recede and the matter is often treated as a minor inconvenience rather than a really big deal. Meanwhile, the truth is, while facing the bar exam, the matter looks quite different and the pressures are incredibly stifling and overbearing.

Given all this angst about the bar exam, some assert it isn't perhaps as realistic and pointed as it ought to be. In a sense, some argue it isn't rough enough and tough enough, at least with respect to what the practice of law truly entails.

Let's consider the future of the bar exam, especially in light of ongoing advances in technology.

Recent trends suggest that the administration of bar exams is aiming to increasingly be undertaken online and via a computer-based proctoring approach. By-and-large, most jurisdictions are still primarily paper-based and involve going to a designated centralized location to take the bar exam in-person. The pandemic has spurred and accelerated overall interest in trying out online methods as a potentially viable alternative.

Going online though is not a friction-free path. There are avid concerns that taking the bar exam online might be discriminatory for those that do not have the needed equipment and nor Internet bandwidth to seamlessly take the exam, plus there are expressed qualms about the possibility of glitches and electronic transmission issues that can permeate any such online endeavor.

For the moment, consider the added possibilities that a computer-based administered bar exam proffers, regardless of whether accessed remotely online or perhaps undertaken in a centralized locale that has computers or portals provided for use during the exam.

Besides the obvious fact that a computer-based exam allows for easier collection of the responses by the exam takers, there is also the added benefit of leveraging computer processing in a real-time manner.

Thinking outside the box, suppose that the capabilities of Artificial Intelligence (AI) are advanced to the degree that there is some semblance of AI-based Legal Reasoning (AILR) that can be achieved via computer systems. Imagine that the AILR is good enough to be deployed as a kind of interrogator, as it were, during the taking of a bar exam.

To what end, you might be wondering?

Let's unpack this and see.

Infusing AI Into The Bar Exam

The traditional means of taking the bar exam consists of the test taker simply reading questions or examining essay prompts and then either writing out a lengthy reply or selecting choices from multiple answers as provided in the test booklet. This is certainly a tried-and-true method of design for the bar exam.

Unfortunately, the result is that the test graders are ultimately only able to assess post-exam what the taker has stated. There is no opportunity to inquire of the taker in any interactive fashion to further ferret out their thinking or basis for the answers indicated. In real life, an aspiring attorney is expected to be able to fluidly interact with judges, fellow attorneys, opposing counsel, clients, and the like.

Overall, a traditional bar exam lacks any grading or assessment associated with how an attorney might be able to act on their toes, including having to cogently be responsive in real-time when making their cases.

One way to gauge the real-time acumen of bar exam test-takers would be to have existing lawyers present or available online and have them participate directly in the testing process by asking questions of the test takers (for which these so included lawyers would presumably be carefully selected and trained to take part in the testing). The designated lawyers would interact with the test takers and be able to inquire, perhaps grill, the nascent legal beagles as to their semblance of intelligence about the law.

Sounds great, though not especially feasible per se. The logistics for such an arrangement would be quite onerous, the cost likely would be through the roof, and there would be an inherent danger that the lawyers serving in such a capacity might be inconsistent and inadvertently imbue the test-taking with a slew of undesirable human foibles and biases (inappropriately steering the grading).

Into the picture steps the use of computer-based AI-enabled legal reasoning or AILR.

A bar exam could be augmented via the crafting of an AI-powered legal reasoning system. Assuming that the bar exam was being given via a computer-based capability, whether online or via computers at a centralized testing locale, the AI would be running on the computers and be integrated into the bar exam materials and process.

Test takers would interact with the AILR during the bar exam.

In addition to the test taker interacting in writing with the AILR, the use of the AI capability would open the opportunity to allow for oral interactions too. Think of the use of Natural Language Processing (NLP), akin to but superior to the likes of Alexa or Siri, which would enable the test takers to carryon an oral dialogue with the AI.

A give-and-take kind of discussion would be performed, allowing the AI to not only ask pre-canned questions and seek predetermined answers (such as the case of multiple-choice questions) but be able to go much further and probe the legal mindedness of the test taker and attempt to ascertain how well they can interactively showcase their presumed legal knowledge.

An Example From A Bar Exam

To give this discussion added tangibility, consider an essay question used on the California Bar Exam earlier this year that subsequently was routinely posted publicly afterward with other facets of the February 2020 test and included some sample answers (anonymized).

The topic entailed contracts law:

"Barn Exports hired Sam, an up-and-coming artist whose work was recently covered in Modern Buildings Magazine, to paint a one-of-a-kind artistic design along the border of the ceiling in its newly renovated lobby. After discussing the work, Ed, the president of Barn, and Sam signed a mutually drafted handwritten contract, which states in its entirety: Sam shall paint a unique design along the entire ceiling border of all public areas of the first-floor lobby. Barn shall pay $75,000 upon completion of the work."

Briefly, the remainder of the prompt describes several aspects that went somewhat awry, such as Ed subsequently telling Sam that he would need to sand and seal the plaster ceiling before painting it, for which Sam believed was not within the scope of the handwritten contract (Sam opted to do the sanding and sealing, anyway, and then added $3,000 to the cost). At the presumed end of the project, turns out that Sam did not paint two public restrooms that were in the lobby, and so Barn Exports refused to make the payment on the work. And so on.

Sam sued Barn Exports for breach of contract, and Barn Exports countersued for specific performance to have the bathrooms painted.

The bar exam asks the test takers to analyze the case and explain the legal underpinnings of the case. For those of you that are already attorneys, put yourself into the shoes of those budding lawyers sitting for the California Bar Exam and envision what your answer would be to this essay question.

I'll give you a moment to contemplate the matter.

Did you feel like you were back in law school and taking a bar exam?

Maybe that is too chilling and brings forth unappealing memories, so let's just move forward with this as an example of how an AI-based legal reasoning system could be included in the testing process.

A written answer submitted by one test taker indicated that as a legal matter the scenario encompassed a services contract and so was governed by common law.

Imagine an AILR component that could dialogue with the respondent and ask, for example, whether Article II of the Uniform Commercial Code might apply to this situation. Doing so would engage the test taker in considering whether the UCC might apply (and explain why it would not), and possibly get them to reconsider whether the common law answer is the prevailing reply. This would force onto the surface aspects that otherwise are not present per se in any static and non-interactive test-taking response.

Another opportunity for dialogue arises when the sample written response pointed out that consideration must be present for there to be a valid contract. Helpfully, the test taker then elaborated that a showing of consideration is done by the facts evidencing that the parties have obtained a legal benefit or detriment as a result of the contract. This is a handy generic response. The AILR could inquire as to what the apparent *actual* benefit or detriment might be in this case, such as for Barn Exports and also for Sam.

As such, notice that the AILR could conduct a discussion toward assessing the conceptual aspects of the law as understood by the test taker (comparing common law to the UCC), or can go in the direction of the applied aspects of the law (seeking specifics in this case of the benefits or detriments associated with the matter). The AILR could also try to fakeout the test taker, such as seeming to assert something that is not a lawful posture and thus expect that the respondent ought to refute the point.

Range Of AI Capabilities To Be Leveraged

Depending upon how far out there we want the AILR to go, consider some additional possibilities, such as the use of interactive role-playing in a legal context:

- The AI could pretend or simulate the role of a judge and have a discussion in that judicial mode with the test taker about the case at hand.

- The AI could act as a fellow attorney that was working with the test taker and wanted to confer about the case.

- The AI could simulate the efforts of an opposing attorney that was fighting on one side, let's say representing Barn Exports, while the test taker is asked to serve as the attorney for Sam.

- The AI could simulate either of the parties of the case, such as pretending to be Ed, and the test taker would be asked to be the attorney for Ed and explain to him which laws pertain and do so in a manner that a non-legal trained person would comprehend.

You might be under the assumption that the AI would do these interactions in a dispassionate and rather robotic way. With advances in NLP, the interaction could be programmed to act in a more human-like manner and incorporate emotionally laden conveyances. For example, the simulation of being a judge might be accompanied by just a taste of some harshness, something that can assuredly occur in the real world as sometimes exhibited when attorneys in a case appear to be ill-prepared or unresponsive to courtroom inquiries. In that sense, the test taker is not only dealing with the words and meaning of the law, they would also contend with the stresses of being in the practice of law.

If you believe that this kind of inquiry would be advantageous for ascertaining the licensing of future lawyers, keep that sentiment in mind as it is something gradually and seemingly inexorably that will likely arise.

For those that believe this would be untenable and overinflate what a bar exam is intended to achieve, the good news for you is that this kind of AI is still years away from fruition. There are lesser variants of computer-based testing that can do simpler versions of this type of interaction, and could be considered sooner rather than later, but the full-blown AILR is not in the cards for now.

Conclusion

One question I often get asked is whether there will even be a need to use bar exams in the future whence AILR exists since one prophecy is that we won't need human lawyers once that day arrives. I'm not quite as convinced about that wholescale replacement of human lawyers with AILR, and, in any case, the AILR could be less proficient than a human lawyer and still partake in this kind of interactive interrogator capacity.

Probably makes you glad that you passed the bar before the days of AI intervention arrive.

Note: *For supplemental materials depicting the aspects discussed in this chapter, refer to Appendix B, which contains various augmented diagrams, charts, and additional related facets of relevance.*

CHAPTER 5

AI & LAW:
AI-BASED ADJUDICATION DISPASSIONATE

Key briefing points about this essay:

- Tremendous effort has gone into the exploration of how judges think

- A longstanding assertion is that judges should set aside all emotion and sentimentality

- Meanwhile, lately, there has been criticism that AI-based legal systems will lack emotion

- This begs the question of whether AI is better or worse off as a dispassionate judge

- Though the added twist is that AI can indeed be infused with emotion if we so desire

Introduction

A lot of thought has gone into thinking about how judges think. Any attorney worth their salt is always eyeing the judges they will encounter, doing so to try and size-up what kind of rulings and adjudication dalliances a particular judge will likely undertake.

Legal scholars have carefully probed the minds of judges and attempted to ferret out what goes on inside their heads.

Thomas Hobbes wrote in his famous 1651 treatise entitled *Leviathan* that judges should divest themselves of all fear, anger, hatred, love, and compassion. In 2005, the future-seated Supreme Court Justice John Roberts espoused that judges should use "dispassionate thinking," though he also acknowledged and lamented that doing so is much harder than it might seem. Indeed, Roberts starkly revealed that he too has had difficulties setting aside emotions when rendering a final decision in some of the more notably heart-tugging and gut-wrenching judicial cases that had come before him.

All told, there is a lengthy history of touting that judges are supposed to be dispassionate in their judicial machinations. This goal of being wholly objective and utterly devoid of emotional sway is stated by some as an absolute requirement for any and all judges and held high as an ideal that must be continuously observed and stridently achieved. Judges that allow the infusion of passion or emotion into their judicial decision-making are said to be undercutting the core precepts of how our esteemed judicial process and system are supposed to properly operate.

Whether this ideal is viable remains unabashedly debated, internally so within the legal profession, and likewise captures the attention of the public at large about what is the role and behavior expected of judges.

Can we reasonably expect a judge to be a fully dispassionate judicial decider?

According to comments made by Supreme Court Justice Jackson in his dissenting opinion of the 1944 case of the *United States v. Ballard*, he associated the notion of dispassionate judges to the likes of Santa Claus and the Easter bunnies. Perhaps there is no sensible way to separate the emotions that a judge has from the analytical and logic-based cognitive judicial reasoning that are used when deciding a court case. We might be fooling ourselves into believing that passion or emotion can be held at arm's length and not allowed into the judicial envelope.

Pretending that dispassionate judging can occur is tantamount to (trigger alert) feigning that Santa Claus is real.

So, this unending spinning wheel keeps going, trying to gauge whether passion can be pushed aside, meanwhile rotating immediately back to the view that emotion is ever-present and inextricably intertwined into the somber act of judging.

Some propose that the most appropriate way to frame or scope this consideration is by emphasizing the importance of the "emotionally intelligent" judge, whereby all judges should be trained in and become versed in how to best control and channel their emotional and passion-filled leanings. This suggests that judges would then realize the significant influence that their sentimentality entails, and would have a well-honed means to corral it (something that seasoned judges might discover over years of judicial practice, but via formal training be gleaned more systematically rather than in today's decidedly ad hoc manner).

AI And The Sentimentality Of Judges

Let's shift gears for a moment and then tie this discussion to the future of the law.

There are ongoing efforts to advance Artificial Intelligence (AI) into the field of law. It is assumed that proficient and legally-fluent AI Legal Reasoning (AILIR) will eventually be crafted and become deployed on state-of-the-art computer systems, making use of the latest in Natural Language Processing (NLP), Machine Learning (ML), Deep Learning (DL), and the like. We can expect to see the use of AILR as embedded into and supplementing the myriad of other advances in the LegalTech realm.

One prediction is that we will eventually make use of AI-based "robo-judges" (a so-called robot judge is a phrasing that I've previously exhorted is overused and ought to be averted, though unfortunately it is admittedly an instantly recognizable wording and has already gained demonstrative popularity).

A fascinating paper in the *Stanford Technology Law Review* last year by Richard Re and Alicia Solow-Niederman on "Developing Artificially Intelligent Justice" explores the topic of AI-based adjudication.

The overall notion is that there will likely be AI-based adjudication and thus potentially reduce the need for human judges, either by working hand-in-hand with human judges and reducing their workload or by the AI itself directly tackling adjudication on its own. Depending upon how far you are willing to carry that torch, the presumed endpoint is that there will no longer be any human judges in our court systems and the act of judicial decision-making will be the exclusive and utterly sole preserve of the AI that we've all put into place.

Never going to happen, some exclaim.

When asked why this won't occur, one exerted response is that the AI-based judicial decision-making system will not have the passion and emotion that human judges imbue, and we would be handing over our judicial fates to a dispassionate machine.

Whoa, take another look at that argument for why AI-based adjudication isn't going to fly. The assertion is that the AI will lack the passion and emotions of humanity, therefore we must reject the use of this dispassionate-oriented computer-based approach. But, of course, as mentioned earlier in this discussion, the assumption has seemingly all along been that we want judges to be dispassionate.

After all of that enduring angst and teeth grinding about how to get judges to distance themselves from their emotions, lo and behold a means to do so arises, presumably via the AI-based judging apparatus and the excising of human judges from the adjudication matter. In theory, we ought to eagerly be seeking to put in place such AI-based capabilities.

Doing so would appear to solve a long-time paradoxical problem that has stood the test of time by its resoluteness of being unsolvable.

A somewhat sheepish response by some is that they didn't expect nor intend to toss out the baby with the bathwater, as it were. They wanted a means to suppress or curtail the human presence of passion or emotions and did not desire to wholescale discard the human element entirely in that vaunted quest. Others retort that you can't have it both ways. You either accept that human emotion is going to enter into the picture if you opt to use human judges, or otherwise if you want the passion to be extinguished you'll have no choice but to yank the human judge out of the adjudication arena.

In short, the argument being made is that since the AI lacks emotion, it ought not to be judging (or so it is asserted).

Another separate and alternative twist of this argument is that the proposed AI-based judging mechanisms cannot possibly replicate the capabilities of human judges without also embodying passions and emotions.

This is a trickier posture. Here's how it goes. We all would seem to concur that humans have emotions. We would seem to concur that human *judges* have emotions, as per the fact that they are humans. Perhaps judging can only be satisfactorily or sufficiently undertaken by human judges, warts, and all (i.e., with their passions and emotions), and thus the judging act requires a semblance or a necessary ingredient consisting of emotion or passion.

Using that kind of logic, and if it is the case that the AI-based adjudication systems won't have emotions or passions, the ironclad argument is that they would fail to render suitable judicial decisions, no matter what they tried to undertake. The judicial decisions would be perniciously unlike that of human judges and therefore we ought to not fall into a mental trap of believing that the AI can do so.

It does seem a bit ironic to pull the (metaphorical) passion-instilled *rabbit out of a hat* to make the case for why AI-based judges won't cut the mustard.

There is a counterargument that few seem to be including into their calculus on this particular attempt to pushback at the AI-based adjudication. First, let's go ahead and accept the premise that there is a divine ringing of the bells of a necessary role for passion and emotion in the judging effort. As you are about to see, this lays a bit of a snare.

The surprising revelation perhaps is that there are efforts underway of adding a semblance of emotion or passion into the inner workings of AI systems. Some AI researchers fervently believe that we can capture the same essence underlying emotions and passions of humans by computationally encapsulating those attributes. If you want an AI system that will get angry, or be happy, or display compassion, this can be arranged. No problem.

Where this takes us is to the fact that if you really do think that judges can only do judging by having passions and emotions, which maybe they put to the side momentarily or maybe they are nonetheless swayed by, an AI-based adjudicator can be made likewise to have those characteristics.

In a sense, you can have your cake and eat it too.

One bonus aspect might be that the AI-based judicial decision-making could be overtly dialed-up or dialed-down in terms of the passion or emotion that we want it to incorporate (a much harder facility for human judges). Furthermore, you could presumably get the AI to readily divulge how much of its judicial decision was immersed in emotion or passion, thus being above-board about how such qualities affected the adjudication itself. For those of you that are worried that this infusing of passion and emotion into the AI is a bad idea, well, in theory, the dial could be set to zero and those added elements would not play a role at all.

And for those of you that are crestfallen that this saving grace of not having emotions was the ace in the deck to prevent AI judges from being fostered upon us all, there is a remaining crack or opening in the matter to give you some hope.

You could contend that the "artificial" formulation of emotion and passion is fakery and not equivalent to the true and heartfelt version of human emotion and passion. As such, a computationally modeled variant is woefully inferior and nothing more than a cheap ploy to distract and overcome a more bona fide stance.

Conclusion

One thing is for sure, namely that there are a lot of emotions and passion surrounding the question of whether human judges can detach themselves from their sentiments, and in the future, there will undoubtedly be as much intensity and fervor over the advent of AI-based adjudication.

Note: *For supplemental materials depicting the aspects discussed in this chapter, refer to Appendix B, which contains various augmented diagrams, charts, and additional related facets of relevance.*

CHAPTER 6

AI & LAW:

BIGLAW

Key briefing points about this essay:

- Law firms of any notable size are especially tricky to manage and ably adjust to market shifts

- BigLaw is viewed as likely to have internal squabbles over the advent of AI-based legal services

- Some law firms will quickly embrace AI, others will ignore or deflect AI emerging changes

- One prediction is that BigLaw will inexorably have to adapt to and utilize AI or suffer woes

- Thus expect to see BigLaw ultimately grasp onto and embody AI-based legal services

Introduction

Any law firm that is even a modicum of size and scale can be quite challenging to successfully manage. There is the continual tug-of-war over which legal services to provide and whether the chosen set is well suited to ongoing sustenance and potential growth of the firm. Being dependent upon the labor employed to provide said services is equally a nightmare.

Do we have the right number of attorneys, or are we understaffed or overstaffed?

How do we keep the good ones and gently nudge out the sour ones?

Some insist that having to be a leader in a law firm is akin to the legendary chore of trying to herd cats.

For those that like to couch things in a loftier tone, the in's and out's of running a law firm are often compared to the rigors of playing chess. The choices underlying which legal services to be proffered and how to best parlay them is akin to leveraging the pieces on a chessboard, aiming to use whatever strengths you have and trying to avert possible weaknesses. The legal services promulgated must be matched to hoped-for demand from clients and aligned with the resources and legal-beagle steeped capabilities that the firm can suitably bring to the marketplace.

One ongoing question that has nagged the legal profession seemingly forever is the extent to which technology can or ought to be utilized as a strategic and interwoven element into the embodiment of legal services.

At first glance, some contend that the spate of law profession tech has a mere backroom purpose and requires scant attention. This relatively narrow mindset usually entails making sure that the legal teams have just sufficient tech in-hand such as word processing, spreadsheets, and some semblance of online access, at a barebones capacity, and otherwise LegalTech is considered an unappealing and undesirable cost that has to be kept to a rock-bottom minimum.

Others take a wider perspective and see LegalTech as increasingly being instrumental to their legal efforts, encompassing not meager background proclivities but also standing at the forefront of what the firm undertakes and how it presents itself to the world. The tension or strain between perceiving legal-oriented tech as a low-value high-cost investment versus being a high-value ROI-justifiable one is an ongoing form of angst and struggle within most law firms today.

AI As A Game Changer

Suppose we toss into the game a kind of interloper, namely AI.

Artificial Intelligence (AI) is gradually being advanced and bolstering the capabilities of modern LegalTech. The use of AI's Natural Language Processing (NLP) facilities is making strides in aiding e-Discovery, along with boosting the manner and ease of drafting or analyzing legal contracts, and so on. Machine Learning (ML) and Deep Learning (DL) have especially pushed forward in the legal realm. These computationally sophisticated modeling features can do data related pattern matching that is leveraged when searching for appropriate precedents in a large corpus of court cases and otherwise stridently augments prior and cruder methods of making such queries.

Most would agree that AI in the law is going to proceed apace and in fact, accelerate over time. Though today's AI is still relatively simplistic and not a hallmark game-changer per se, as yet, the belief is that AI will noticeably improve and be further extended and applied to the field of law. Eventually and inevitably, there will be a threshold reached at which AI in the law becomes a crucial must-have instead of an optional take-it or leave-it proposition.

In short, there will be some law firms that opt to get on board with adopting and using AI, including infusing state-of-the-art AI-based LegalTech into their ongoing and possibly expanding set of legal services offerings, and meanwhile other law firms that will choose to do the classic wait-and-see, dragging their feet until the friction of not using AI becomes so hot that something breaks the stalemate.

Let's consider how this envisioned future will impact BigLaw.

Presumably, for those BigLaw members that end up embracing AI, they will wrap the capabilities into their legal services and benefit accordingly, assuming they do so smartly and with chess-like shrewdness.

Predictions are that the AI-powered LegalTech will imbue AI Legal Reasoning (AILR) of a semi-autonomous nature, later on advancing to be autonomous realm, and thus can undertake various legal-oriented tasks. This initiative will mean that human lawyers can be more productive as a result of using the AILR, similar to using a backhoe instead of a hand trowel, or in the case of playing chess, it would be analogous to having an AI-based chess master at your side, being available at all times and able to conduct legal analyses and offer a modicum of legal acumen.

The legal teams of human attorneys would be more productive and able to take on more cases and deeper cases than via today's methods. They would be able to speed-up their legal work. The AILR would also provide a secondary double-check, being able to point out potential legal gotchas, omissions, or other weaknesses or even failings in the legal case efforts underway.

If that envisioned future arises, the question then logically comes up as to whether that adoption of AI will be a competitive differentiator or not.

In other words, for those BigLaw that do adopt AI, would they be rewarded by the marketplace for having done so? If not, it would seem to showcase that the BigLaw that has not chosen to immerse AI into their offerings have apparently made the better choice, doing so by presumably foregoing the cost and effort of such adoption and remain seemingly unscathed by the market.

One assertion is that clients will indubitably react to those law firms that indeed have AI versus those that do not have AI.

Clients Going Where AI Is

Here's the thinking involved.

A client is trying to decide which BigLaw to choose for conducting needed legal efforts.

Assume that this involves an assessment or evaluation of what the BigLaw candidate firms can provide, entailing the types of legal services, the depth of those legal services, the availability of those legal services, the cost of those legal services, and so on.

If the case can be made that the AI-powered legal services are potentially less costly, and at an equal level of quality, perhaps even higher quality due to the double-checking enabled by the AI, this naturally gives those AI-adopters an added competitive edge. Ergo, clients of a mindfully discerning bent would likely realize this significant difference and amply consider it, seriously and with keen import.

There is also the potential sense of image or cachet too. Those BigLaw firms with the AI embellished instrumentality will be able to portray their firm as more up-to-date and earnestly seeking ways to improve their legal services offerings. That alone can be a substantive demarcation, even if the AI embodiment does not necessarily rise to an overtly demonstrative force in how their legal services are being rendered.

You could argue that those of the BigLaw without AI in its midst will hence be at an aching disadvantage, distinctly so.

Clients would potentially instead choose a competitor, one that has acclimated itself to AI Legal Tech. Also, a clever negotiating ploy by clients might be that a prospective (or existing) client ought to get better pricing since the BigLaw non-adopter of AI has not had to bear the costs of getting up-to-speed on AI. Furthermore, the non-adopter will seemingly not be able to competitively match the pricing that the AI-adopters can achieve, and thus any bid by the non-adopter is inherently suspect as being overpriced (or, can be claimed as such, in a chess-like bluffing gambit).

You might be wondering why this would happen to solely the BigLaw firms and not also reach into the rest of the law entities pool.

Some hypothesize that the modest-sized and smaller law firms will somehow get a momentary free pass on the matter. The assumption is that clients will realize that the cost of AI adoption is not viable for those petite-sized entities and those such clients will graciously look the other way accordingly. It would seem doubtful that this veritable get-out-of-jail-free card would last very long.

As such, your instincts that ostensibly this matter will confront smaller and even the smallest of law firms seem justifiably credible. In that sense, law firms of all sizes will be vulnerable to the AI adoption calculus, and therefore you can substitute BigLaw with something like AllLaw in the preceding discourse.

Perhaps most notably, one viewpoint is that the AI will be part-and-parcel of using any LegalTech tools. In that manner, and based on the variety of pricing options by the AI touting LegalTech vendors, just about any law firm would find the AI capabilities relatively affordable. If that particular prophecy comes true, it has other somewhat potentially earth-shattering impacts in the legal profession. For example, perhaps the playing field becomes leveled across all law firms and the AI capabilities turn the industry on its head.

Here's the kicker:

> The existence of a BigLaw evaporates as a premise, meanwhile, the nature of using legal services becomes a highly fragmented business with no particular advantage for being a larger collective versus a smaller or loosely federated assembly.

One supposes that this blasphemous scenario is something of great wear-and-tear upon the minds of those leading BigLaw. How are they to cope in such a predicament? Will they get boxed in, and ultimately be boxed out too?

All in all, much teeth grinding seems to be in store.

Conclusion

Of course, all of this is not yet a reality, and whether it is a dream, perhaps a scary one, or perhaps a treasured one, depends upon your stance concerning AI, the legal profession, and the proffering of legal services. To ensure that every lawyer and law partner stays awake at night thinking about these future events, consider the outsized possibility that AI Legal Reasoning will become so autonomous that no human barristers are needed at all. Imagine how that would change the legal profession.

With that being said, time to go get another strong cup of coffee and get back to the day-to-day work of practicing the law, and set aside, albeit briefly, what the future of AI and law holds.

――――――

Note: *For supplemental materials depicting the aspects discussed in this chapter, refer to Appendix B, which contains various augmented diagrams, charts, and additional related facets of relevance.*

CHAPTER 7

AI & LAW:

CANONS OF CONTRADICTION

Key briefing points about this essay:

- Attorneys generally seek to craft the strongest possible argument favoring their side of a case

- The human foible of anchoring to your own posture can undermine the strength of an argument

- Best to always keep in mind the legendary *canons of construction* by legal scholar Llewellyn

- Another perspective is to consider these as mindful *canons of contradiction*

- These canons raise interesting prospects and potential difficulties for AI-enabled legal reasoning

Introduction

May the stronger argument rue the day.

That is the foundational keystone for our adversarial approach to the law. Two sides pitted against each other, each putting forth the best and most compelling argument that they can muster.

Presumably, a judge then has the task of assessing the competing arguments and ascertaining which has made the most convincing or persuasive case.

Attorneys are trained to assemble a legal argument that will seek to prevail. Indeed, for most lawyers, there is a kind of joyous satisfaction upon having arduously and with oodles of sweat and tears crafted an argument that they believe, in their heart of hearts, shines brightly and rises above all other possible argument-making contenders.

One ominous difficulty that many fresh-faced attorneys discover early in their legal career is the oft tendency to anchor to your own set of arguments for a given court case. You carefully craft the legal position for your side of the ledger and sometimes become overly enamored of what great beauty you hath doth created. It is hard to give equal weight to whatever the opposing side argument might potentially be.

Of course, getting caught ill-prepared or unawares about what the other side has developed for their legal posturing is tantamount to being behind the eight ball and proffers foreboding tidings for your case. In theory, you ought to have completely anticipated the opposing position and therefore ensured that your legal treatise has already dealt with and dispatched those sharply pointed attacks amid their own beauteous set of arguments and counterarguments.

This notion of attempting to divine beforehand the likely legal stance of your opponent was eloquently stated by John Stuart Mill in his legendary *On Liberty* from 1859: "He who knows only his own side of the case knows little of that. His reasons may be good, and no one may have been able to refute them. But if he is equally unable to refute the reasons on the opposite side; if he does not so much as know what they are, he has no ground for preferring either opinion. Nor is it enough that he should hear the arguments of adversaries from his own teachers, and accompanied by what they offer as refutations. He must be able to hear them from the persons who actually believe them; who defend them in earnest, and do their very utmost for them."

Notice that not only does that sage advice indicate that you need to anticipate the position of the opposing side, there is a strident urging that you must somehow see or grasp their position as it is fervently believed and voraciously composed by the other side.

This is a vital point.

Newbie attorneys or sloppy seasoned ones are apt to dreamily envision a milquetoast version of what the opposing side is presumably going to formulate. It is easier to pretend or fool oneself into thinking that the opposition is going to blow it and underwhelm when it comes to developing their arguments. Those legal wimps will for sure miss the key points and put forth a laughable legal pose, one so supposes. In that case, there is no particular need to agonizingly scrutinize your legal arguments since the other side is going to falter and be vacuous anyway.

It is energy sapping to try and put yourself into the shoes of the opposing counsel and thus a lackadaisical cognitive trick is to delude yourself into assuming that you've got it right and they have gotten it wrong. Unfortunately, this is bound to haunt you once their position becomes known. There is a famous line that says the more you sweat in training, the less you bleed in battle, for which all barristers ought to sternly observe and keep at the forefront of their legal mindset.

Utilizing AI-Enabled Legal Argumentation

How can you bolster your adversarial acumen to be more demonstrative?

In a prior article, I had discussed that AI-based legal argumentation will gradually become a handy means for lawyers to prepare themselves for their courtroom brawls. In a sense, the AI will simulate the role of an opposing attorney and thus allow a robust tit-for-tat discourse when preparing for a case. This is akin to having a colleague looking over your shoulder and playing a devil's advocate role to find any loopholes or guffaws in your legal logic.

When I present AI-empowered legal-beagle approaches at webinars and conferences there is an oft-asked question of whether the AI might simply craft an ideal or supreme argument and therefore obviate the need to anticipate any counter posturing. In other words, ask the AI to put together a fully winning argument and then sit back and toss aside any worries about anything the opposing counsel might try to assert.

If judging and adjudication was a purely mathematical milieu, perhaps this kind of AI-optimizing argumentation idealization would be possible. Turns out though that the law, the practice of law, and our courts are imbued with humans and human indeterminism. It is problematic to a priori be able to formulate a legal position that is unassailable and that will attain utter certainty in ruing the day.

An ample example of this indeterminism is vividly illuminated by the research work of Karl Llewellyn and his insightful canons of construction outlined in a 1950 paper published in the *Vanderbilt Law Review*. I cheekily refer to the rules as the canons of *contradiction*.

Eye-Opening Canons Of Contradiction

Let's take a look at a handful of the canons or rules (there are twenty-eight all told), selecting a few especially evidentiary ones for ease of discussion herein. These each depict a lawful posture that involves a point and counterpoint indication.

Textual interpretation

- Position: "A statute cannot go beyond its text."

- Counter position: "To effect its purpose a statue may be implemented beyond its text."

Retroactive effects

- Position: "A statute imposing a new penalty or forfeiture, or a new liability or disability, or creating a new right of action will not be construed as having a retroactive effect."

- Counter position: "Remedial statutes are to be liberally construed and if a retroactive interpretation will promote the ends of justice, they should receive such construction."

Language ambiguity

- Position: "If language is plain and unambiguous it must be given effect."

- Counter position: "Not when literal interpretation would lead to absurd or mischievous consequences or thwart manifest purpose."

Word weighting

- Position: "Every word and clause must be given effect."

- Counter position: "If inadvertently inserted or if repugnant to the rest of the statute, they may be rejected as surplusage."

Those examples showcase that there is not necessarily an optimal solution per se that could be derived from an AI-based legal reasoning system. For each proffered position there is an equal and compelling counter position. None is inherently the superior of the other and it is a time-based and contextually sensitive human-led ascertaining that determines the final winning argument (which, can be later on overturned or rewritten as society evolves and the standing laws are changed or potentially reinterpreted by humanity).

Conclusion

Some believe that we ought to be applying physics to the law, ostensibly figuring out the "laws of nature" that presumably underpin our set of societal laws and how we undertake our adjudication efforts. Perhaps Sir Isaac Newton's famous third law of physics applies in this instance, namely that for every action there is an equal and opposite reaction, albeit for each legal posture there is a potentially equal and opposite legal position.

In the end, assuming that we are still to be judged by human hands and human-made laws, the final arbiter is not some invisible force of gravity or centrifugal energy, but instead, the cognitive legal mindpower possessed by mankind, including the possibility of an extended hand provided by the crafting of AI-amplified legal acumen.

―――――――

Note: *For supplemental materials depicting the aspects discussed in this chapter, refer to Appendix B, which contains various augmented diagrams, charts, and additional related facets of relevance.*

CHAPTER 8

AI & LAW:

PAPERCLIP MAXIMIZER QUALMS

Key briefing points about this essay:

- Paperclips have more importance than might be apparent to the ordinary eye

- Turns out that a parable involving paperclips has been an AI "hot topic" for many years

- Suppose an AI system went overboard and made paperclips obediently but to our detriment

- This same unintentional adverse consequence could befall the use of AI in the law

- Knowing about the paperclip predicament can help guide AI adoption in the legal field

Introduction

Excuse me, do you perchance have a paperclip handy?

Any discussion about paperclips would generally seem to be unheralded, other than the routine request for a paperclip or the polite handing over of a paperclip or two to a colleague.

We regularly use those curvy shapes of metal in our daily efforts and yet they don't get any special attention or consideration.

A paperclip is undeniably handy when you have various legal papers that need to be readily bunched together, but otherwise, the everyday and ostensibly mundane paperclip gets little due. You might find of idle interest that there are about 11 billion paperclips purchased in the United States each year and that this comes out to an average of around 34 paperclips per person. That's nothing to write home about and seems like an abundantly unnecessary cluttering of facts and figures into your otherwise pristine and law-filled legal beagle mind.

Turns out that the lowly paperclip does have another purpose, namely serving as a crucial cornerstone of an ongoing and altogether acrimonious debate in the field of Artificial Intelligence (AI). Let's take a close look at what all the hee-haw is about and consider too how the mighty paperclip parable impacts the intertwining of AI and the law.

In a now-classic paper published in 2003, philosopher Nick Bostrom of Oxford University conjured up a scenario involving AI that has become quite a kerfuffle. His fictional notion starts with the ordinary paperclip at the center of his tale: "It also seems perfectly possible to have a superintelligence whose sole goal is something completely arbitrary, such as to manufacture as many paperclips as possible, and who would resist with all its might any attempt to alter this goal."

As you can see, he postulates that we might someday have AI that has reached a level beyond that of normal human intelligence, ascending into a realm of so-called superintelligence. For clarification, nobody can say for sure whether this emergence will happen, nor can we currently know for sure what this "superintelligence" will consist of. The matter is merely speculative, make that highly speculative, and lacks any substance of particular grounding or reasoned foundation.

I mention and emphasize this salient facet because the premise of the saga is dependent upon an illusion that does not exist, and for which might not ever exist.

You perhaps recall from your days of mathematics and deductive reasoning that if you craft logic based on a false premise then the consequent conclusion can be equally fanciful and utterly false too. There is a bit of devilishness involved since the conclusion, standing on its own, could indeed *possibly* be valid, we just cannot immediately assume it is, especially when the premise itself is alarmingly false.

Legal argumentation is certainly known to have the same difficulty associated with proffering false premises that lead potentially to legally unsound conclusions, ones that might appear to be bona fide and yet upon in-depth assessment are shown to be bogus.

Anyway, for the moment, let's go along with the idea that there will be an AI that is super-intelligent and will be assigned the goal of making paperclips. It seems that humanity can think of nothing more substantive to have the revered and mankind-invented super-intelligence undertake, such as creating a cure for cancer or somehow achieving world peace and thus instead focus all its super-intelligence on making paperclips.

As will be apparent shortly, turns out that the focus could in fact be on some other weightier matter, so the paperclip aspect is really just a placeholder per se. The crux is that the AI has been given a specific goal and presumably also instructed to pursue that goal at any cost.

Now for the punchline from this philosophical brain-teaser: "Another way for it to happen is that a well-meaning team of programmers make a big mistake in designing its goal system. This could result, to return to the earlier example, in a superintelligence whose top goal is the manufacturing of paperclips, with the consequence that it starts transforming first all of earth and then increasing portions of space into paperclip manufacturing facilities."

The full reveal is that an AI system might someday be commanded to pursue a particular goal and the resulting consequence is that the AI proceeds to grab-up all available resources to attain the stated goal. This has the adverse impact of undermining other elements and could detrimentally end-up usurping everything else in this mindless and blindly obedient quest.

The implication is that ultimately the super-intelligence AI will be so obsessed about producing paperclips that humanity becomes of little or no importance. By following that logic to its endpoint, in theory, the AI would either indirectly kill-off mankind or might even choose to purposely do so, all to achieve the making of paperclips and satisfy the sole-purpose goal.

Notice that the chosen goal, the production of paperclips, could be something else altogether. The emphasis herein is that the goal begets overshadowing any other considerations.

One supposes you could trick your way around this contention by setting the goal to be the enrichment of humanity. In that logical case, the AI would presumably do whatever it could to aid mankind, though this too could be undermined depending upon how this simpleton-minded AI that is labeled as super-intelligent opted to proceed.

Some Gripes About Those Grapes

One gripe about all of this philosophizing is that the alleged super-intelligence is pretty stupid.

How can an AI that has supposedly reached super-intelligence (whatever that is), be so dense and obtuse that it obeys an instruction to achieve a singular and narrow goal? Would we not expect such AI to question what it is being asked to do? Seems like we might hope for a super-intelligence that can achieve better work, perhaps coming up with goals that we aren't even thinking of. This super-intelligence ought to be able to outthink us, and maybe come up with goals that exceed our expectations and ostensibly limited ways of thought.

Another qualm about this scenario is the presumption of a one-and-only-one goal.

Those of you that enjoy science fiction are likely to hark to the writings of Isaac Asimov and his "The Three Laws" postulation in 1942. One of the rules he postulates for robotics and AI is the preservation of mankind.

This is not the only goal.

There are three: "(1) A robot may not injure a human being or, through inaction, allow a human being to come to harm, (2) A robot must obey the orders given it by human beings except where such orders would conflict with the First Law, (3) A robot must protect its own existence as long as such protection does not conflict with the First or Second Law."

It would seem like a super-intelligence would be given a multitude of goals and have to try and balance and attain them in some measured way. The philosophical tale asserts that the programmers of the AI went amok, as it were, and foolishly established a goal-based system that takes only one goal at a time. Not wanting to beat a dead horse but this again seems odd and one wonders how this super-intelligence is any semblance of super-intelligence when those darned programmers can merely do a switcheroo and make the AI into a single goal chaser.

One last point, if you are not enamored of the paperclips in the story, there is an alternative version that some in the AI domain prefer.

For example, you can be a bit loftier by substituting the role of the paperclips with instead a quest to solve the Riemann Hypothesis. The Riemann Hypothesis involves a key question about the nature and distribution of prime numbers. Bernhard Riemann proposed a hypothesis about prime numbers in 1859 and mathematicians have been trying to prove or disprove it ever since.

It is so important that it is considered a vaunted *Millennium Prize Problem* and resides stridently in the same ranks as the computer science quest for whether P=NP problem (a mathematical question that if you can solve would garner you worldwide attention and adulation). Some say that true pure mathematicians are continually slaving away at the Riemann Hypothesis and consider it to be one of the greatest unsolved mathematical puzzles.

So, change up the saga and assume that the AI was told to solve the Riemann Hypothesis and eagerly consumed all of the Earth's resources to achieve this. A more impressive premise than those humble paperclips, but the same result nonetheless.

AI In The Law And Those Paperclips

Shifting gears, consider what this fable has to do with AI and the law.

Here's the rub.

Suppose there is an AI system that is being used by a prosecutor's office. The AI has reached a high enough level of legal reasoning that it has been granted the same capabilities as a human attorney.

Imagine that the head of the prosecutor's office decides to stipulate to the AI that the annual goal for prosecutions in that locale is to achieve a 90% resolution rate.

Okay, we now have an akin scenario and similarly dicey predicament. The AI is presumably assigned one goal. It will seek to achieve that goal, even if it is seemingly nonsensical to do so. What kinds of corner-cutting might the AI undertake to make sure it hits the ninety percent goal? We presumably do not know. In essence, we cannot assume that justice is served merely by the attaining of that particular goal.

This then showcases how the tale of the paperclips can be utilized to act as a warning or caution about the adoption of AI-based legal reasoning systems. We would be imprudent to setup such AI via setting solely a singular goal and for which there is nothing else offsetting or monitoring how that goal is being achieved.

In the instance of a super-intelligent AI, I already harangued that this purported super-intelligence is not very smart if it gets waylaid by a single goal premise.

Switching hats, drop the super-intelligence notion, and concentrate on any kind of AI, including the human intelligence level and the levels below that of human intelligence.

As we proceed forward with the widespread implementation of AI in the law, our eyes ought to be wide open and be watchful for the insidious chance of establishing AI that becomes this sole-goal pursuing miscreant. I would argue that the true human-level intelligence AI would seem unlikely to fall into such a trap, though we don't yet have any kind of AI that approaches that of human cognition. There isn't any AI that has common-sense reasoning and nor any that is within a country mile of sentience.

We do though have AI that is touted as somehow being sentient and astute by marketers and which then reaps bold headlines in the news. This can soften us up and delude us into believing that today's AI would do well in whatever role it might be placed, including acting as legal aid or possibly even serving as a legal advisor outright.

Do not let yourself be misguided by those misrepresentations.

There is yet another helpful lesson about AI and the law to be learned from the paperclip saga. AI specialists urge that whenever AI is used, there needs to be a devised path of what is called *instrumental convergence* toward any vaunted topmost goal. This means that there should be a series of sub-goals that constructively interweave toward achieving the perched overarching goal.

You might for example construe the rules of conduct that attorneys must abide by as a kind of sub-goal safety net in the legal realm. Rather than lawyers getting away with any desired extreme conduct to win a case, there are boundaries and limits established to constrain such wanton efforts. With the advent of AI in the law, we might similarly expect that AI systems will have to adhere to the rules of conduct, potentially adjusted or customized to computer-based AI-based legal reasoning rather than that of human barristers.

Conclusion

All told, the moment you hear or read that AI is coming to the practice of law, remember the fable of the paperclips and be sure that you know what the AI is being set up to accomplish. If you let your guard down, we all might find ourselves drowning in paperclips, frantically swimming to stay atop the AI-based human-devised machinations.

Note: *For supplemental materials depicting the aspects discussed in this chapter, refer to Appendix B, which contains various augmented diagrams, charts, and additional related facets of relevance.*

CHAPTER 9
AI & LAW:
QUESTIONS OF EFFECTIVE AI COUNSEL

Key briefing points about this essay:

- The Sixth Amendment ensures that criminal defendants will have the assistance of legal counsel

- An unstated but implied facet is that such legal counsel will perform in an effective manner

- *Strickland v. Washington* ruling of the Supreme Court laid out the effectiveness parameters

- Some criticize though that the two-parts effectiveness guidelines are overly open-ended

- Effectiveness will remain a vital consideration even in an era of AI-based legal reasoning

Introduction

Imagine that you hire a plumber to do some work on your house. You are adding a new bathroom and sought a professional plumber to get everything properly connected. After the plumber finishes the job, you discover that the bathroom faucet only works intermittently, and water doesn't flow consistently.

Worse still, water from the sink overfills and spills out onto the bathroom floor.

Was the plumber effective in the work performed?

Based on the outcome, we certainly have doubts that this plumber was effective and readily would assert that the plumber was summarily ineffective.

Turns out, while the plumber was doing the work, a mess was made, and the plumber seemed to spend an exorbitant amount of time idly on the phone, exceedingly inattentive to the plumbing task. The work process itself was also ineffective.

All told, we would assess the plumber as being ineffective in *both* the outcome of the work and ineffective in the undertaking of the work.

Shifting gears, let's consider how effectiveness and ineffectiveness arise in a different profession, one of a much greater calling, potentially deciding the fate of people and can demonstrably impact people's lives. I'm referring to lawyers and their role in the legal profession and as an officer of the court.

Let's begin with a look at the Constitution.

It is ostensibly apparent that the Constitution provides for the use of a lawyer for a criminal defendant in the occurrence of criminal prosecutions. Indeed, any straightforward reading of the Sixth Amendment proffers a last-but-not-least assemblage of tail-end words that emphasizes the requirement for the assistance of counsel, as highlighted herein via added bolding and italics: "In all criminal prosecutions, the accused shall enjoy the right to a speedy and public trial, by an impartial jury of the State and district wherein the crime shall have been committed, which district shall have been previously ascertained by law, and to be informed of the nature and cause of the accusation; to be confronted with the witnesses against him; to have compulsory process for obtaining witnesses in his favor, and to have **the *Assistance of Counsel for his defence*.**"

Notice that the wording does not indicate the efficacy of the legal counsel per se.

In essence, there seems to be a bit of a semantics gap.

Can just any legal counsel be provided and if so does the mere act of having legal counsel settle the matter in terms of a constitutionally mandated requirement?

Suppose, for example, a legal counsel is provided but does a lousy job in the defense for the criminal defendant, dropping the ball, failing to properly conduct the case, and otherwise flubs and loses the case by seemingly daftness and being wholly ineffective?

There have been many Supreme Court decisions that attempt to clarify what "the assistance of counsel" fully entails, including and particularly about the need for the effectiveness of legal counsel. In the landmark 1984 case of *Strickland v. Washington*, the Supreme Court made it relatively clear that the defense counsel has to perform in an effective legal manner.

This certainly makes sense since the requirement of having legal counsel could readily be undercut by having a sorely ineffective attorney. It would seem of little value to have legal representation if that representation was bereft of legal acumen and utterly ineffective in the defense of the criminal defendant. This would be quite a loophole and leave such defendants in a lurch, proffering a hollow promise of being presumptively legally armed with counsel.

Despite the indubitable sensibility of the Supreme Court clarifying that the constitutionally mandated assistance of counsel must, in fact, be effective, which is something not seemingly explicitly stated in the Sixth Amendment but for which reasonably could be interpreted as inherently assumed, this nonetheless opens another kind of quagmire or conundrum.

Namely, just what does it mean to be either an effective legal counsel or to be an ineffective one?

A potential qualm is that without having a definitive means of measuring any semblance of an effective counsel versus an ineffective counsel, this lays open the all-to-easy path of appealing nearly any and all criminal cases by criminal defendants. At the drop of a hat, one would assume that any losing criminal defendant would instantly raise the red flag that they had ineffective counsel. The appeals courts would be inundated and possibly overwhelmed with a staggering and infinite series of appeals.

In the *Strickland v. Washington* case, there are essentially two paths toward figuring out whether legal counsel is effective or ineffective. One path consists of the effect upon the case at hand, considered an outcome-oriented criterion. The second path has to do with the efforts per se of the legal counsel and thus examines the process and legal wrangling by the defendant's counsel during the case.

Here's what the Supreme Court said regarding that first path that is outcome-focused: "The Sixth Amendment right to counsel is the right to the effective assistance of counsel, and the benchmark for judging any claim of ineffectiveness must be whether counsel's conduct so undermined the proper functioning of the adversarial process that the trial cannot be relied on as having produced a just result."

This tells us that regardless of whatever happened during the trial, we can somewhat treat that as a black box since the key is that if justice was not served and there was an unjust result then this implies there was ineffective legal counsel at hand.

The burden to showcase this presumed possibility of an unjust result is said to fall upon the shoulders of the defendant: "With regard to the required showing of prejudice, the proper standard requires the defendant to show that there is a reasonable probability that, but for counsel's unprofessional errors, the result of the proceeding would have been different. A reasonable probability is a probability sufficient to undermine confidence in the outcome."

For the second path of ascertaining ineffectiveness, here's an excerpt of the Supreme Court decision about the process or actions of the counsel for the defense: "The proper standard for judging attorney performance is that of reasonably effective assistance, considering all the circumstances. When a convicted defendant complains of the ineffectiveness of counsel's assistance, the defendant must show that counsel's representation fell below an objective standard of reasonableness."

And so there you have it, the now acclaimed two-part test of the effectiveness or ineffectiveness of counsel of a criminal defendant.

Easy peasy and the matter would seem completely settled.

Of course, we know that in reality the matter is not at all settled and there is an incredible amount of gray area into which this semblance of effectiveness versus ineffectiveness falls. If we had a type of laundry list or checklist that was ironclad, it would make things a lot simpler and more measurable. The Supreme Court though stated that there isn't purity of measurement in mind: "The standards do not establish mechanical rules; the ultimate focus of inquiry must be on the fundamental fairness of the proceeding whose result is being challenged."

You might argue that it would be impossible to establish a hard-and-fast set of irrefutable rules to guide us about the effectiveness question. Perhaps it is prudent to leave things somewhat ill-defined, thus enabling flexibility and an open mind whenever considering such matters.

Not everyone agrees that this ought to be so loosely specified. In his dissenting opinion, Justice Marshall abundantly expressed his concerns: "Today, for the first time, this Court attempts to synthesize and clarify those standards. For the most part, the majority's efforts are unhelpful. Neither of its two principal holdings seems to me likely to improve the adjudication of Sixth Amendment claims. And, in its zeal to survey comprehensively this field of doctrine, the majority makes many other generalizations and suggestions that I find unacceptable."

He goes further to explain that there would seem ample opportunity to stipulate the process aspects of legal effectiveness and make those into measurable and standardized characteristics that could presumably be rated or scored: "For example, much of the work involved in preparing for a trial, applying for bail, conferring with one's client, making timely objections to significant, arguably erroneous rulings of the trial judge, and filing a notice of appeal if there are colorable grounds therefor could profitably be made the subject of uniform standards."

Which side of this fence are you on?

Do you think that there isn't any viable way to lay down definitive criteria about the effectiveness versus ineffectiveness aspects, or do you believe that this could assuredly be undertaken and would serve as a useful and telling barometer for all future legal counsel?

On a related note, some have quipped that this effectiveness versus ineffectiveness issue is being treated in a binary fashion. Just as a binary digit is either zero or one, or light is either on or off, there appears to be a tendency to assume that a legal counsel is either entirely and exclusively effective or is entirely and exclusively ineffective. The real-world might be that there are gradients around which the balance between effectiveness and ineffectiveness are floating, upon which a plausible assessment can be made for landing on either one (perhaps similar to Schrodinger's cat).

There is also the point made that the effectiveness seems to be a minimum threshold and only suggests sufficiency. If a legal counsel just barely claws their way into the effectiveness camp, they are free and clear. But what about rising above the effectiveness and into the superb, or the exemplary, or even all the way to the top pinnacle of being ideal. The other side has that same status, whereby one can be ineffective and this could range from mildly deficient to entirely worst-possible.

Let's go with a general view about effectiveness versus ineffective of legal counsel in criminal cases and refer to this as the overarching *effectiveness milieu*.

We know that the effectiveness milieu applies to today's attorneys.

Today's attorneys are human.

There are predictions that we will eventually and inevitably witness the emergence of Artificial Intelligence (AI) that will be on par with human attorneys and be able to provide autonomous AI legal reasoning. Please be aware that there aren't any such AI-based systems currently and the road to that future is a long and arduous one with lots of potholes and gut-wrenching ruts along the way.

Assuming that we do end-up with AI-based legal reasoning systems that can proffer legal advice to the same degree as human lawyers, this provides some rather substantial food-for-thought about the question surrounding the effectiveness versus ineffectiveness of legal counsel.

One viewpoint is that the AI will be absolutely perfect at the law and therefore there is no longer any need to contemplate any semblance of effectiveness or ineffectiveness. Under this guise, if a criminal defendant is represented by an AI-based legal reasoning system for their criminal defense, they can rest assured that the AI will never make any guffaws and will always decidedly be on the effectiveness side of the coin.

Perhaps this idealization of AI comes from science fiction movies or maybe is based on Utopian visions of the future, but I wouldn't hold my breath on this brash assumption.

Keep in mind that the existing goal of AI is to achieve computer-based intelligence that is the equivalent of human intelligence. We already know and seem to freely agree that human intelligence is subject to falling below effectiveness and landing in the mushy swamp of ineffectiveness. In that case, if the AI is working on a basis comparable to human intelligence, we ought to ergo anticipate that the AI will have foibles and potentially be at times ineffective just as humans can be.

Going with that thought for the moment, this suggests that we will still need to once again deal with the effectiveness versus ineffectiveness question, even in an era of AI-based autonomous legal reasoning systems.

Should we hold the AI to the same loosey-goosey groundwork used to assess human lawyers on legal effectiveness?

Perhaps the advent of AI will push us towards being more definitive about the effectiveness and ineffectiveness criteria. It could be that the emergence of autonomous AI-based legal reasoning systems will spur our attention to this altogether thorny topic. Imagine that the courts come up with something more akin to a detailed checklist and a well-crafted standard about being effective in providing legal counsel.

The next head-scratcher is whether this criterion would apply only to the AI-based legal reasoning systems or would also apply to human attorneys too.

Maybe it would, maybe it wouldn't.

Or there might be a special list for the humans and a different list for the AI systems. That doesn't though necessarily appear to be equitable. Why make that distinction? Perhaps AI-based legal reasoning systems might contest the use of disparate criteria (or the human lawyers might).

Let's add another twist to the dilemma.

We are once again making an implicit assumption of a binary nature, namely that a criminal defendant will have either a human lawyer or an AI-based one.

These are not mutually exclusive conditions. In that sense, there is a false dichotomy hiding in this jungle.

There might very well be the instance of human attorneys that are joined by the amplified efforts of fellow counsel consisting of AI-based legal reasoning capabilities.

While in a courtroom, the human lawyer consults with the AI-based system or vice versa. They work hand-in-hand, as it were.

Does that do away with the question about effectiveness versus ineffectiveness?

Nope, for sure it does not.

Presumably, a criminal defendant could be represented by ineffective legal counsel, albeit being served by a combined mixture of a human lawyer and an augmented AI-based legal reasoning system. The reasoning about this possible adverse consequence is logically deducible. If you had two human attorneys working together, they both could be ineffective, either individually or on the whole. If we are assuming that the AI would be of the equal capability to human attorneys, the replacement of one human for one AI in a pairing is not a guarantee of anything raising above ineffectiveness.

Well, you might be pained to think that AI will be ever able to do what human attorneys can do. Either that will never happen, or at least it won't happen until far beyond the years that those of us alive today will still be on this earth.

It would seem that the future, however you see it, will not obviate the value for and nor the need to have the means to ascertain the effectiveness of counsel. The future might extend or lead to a greater specification on such matters, yet not preclude them entirely.

Conclusion

That seems to be relatively inarguable, perchance the aforementioned points appear to you to be vociferously effective rather than intolerably ineffective.

Note: *For supplemental materials depicting the aspects discussed in this chapter, refer to Appendix B, which contains various augmented diagrams, charts, and additional related facets of relevance.*

CHAPTER 10

AI & LAW:

MULTIJURISDICATIONAL LAWYERING

Key briefing points about this essay:

- There are existing state-by-state admissions requirements for attorneys wishing to switch states

- Some assert that the matter is byzantine, unorderly, unnecessary, and a legal morass

- Multijurisdictional arguments are in camps: Open borders, strict borders, permeable borders

- Consider that eventually and some believe inevitably there will be AI-based legal reasoning

- AI-based legal reasoning will be incrementally devised and has multijurisdictional ramifications

Introduction

You are a seasoned attorney and have built a substantial law practice in upstate New York. After years of enduring the cold winters, you have decided that you would like to relocate to a sunnier state, perhaps Florida, Arizona, California, or any state that has a year-round preponderance of warmer weather.

85

It would certainly be nice to simply take your shingle with you and move to one of those states, immediately being able to continue your legal beagle activities there. Turns out that some of the states you are interested in will allow you to plop down and get to your legal efforts right away, while others have an onerous set of requirements as though you've never practiced law a day in your life.

That is the existing conundrum facing attorneys that want to perform legal work in other states, either doing so permanently, or temporarily, or do so as they have cause to do so, possibly rendering their legal services online and to whichever locale they perchance grab a chunk of work from.

Multijurisdictional lawyering tends to be a maddening topic. There is a sharply divided debate on the matter and seemingly no steadfast resolution to the issue. As we all know, each state has its own way of deciding the requirements for being admitted to the practice of law in that particular state.

It all seems on the surface as relatively straightforward and plainly laid out. You figure out what the hurdles are in terms of needed tests and the like, perform them as needed, and voila, you can practice law in that state. Easy peasy.

Of course, the problem is that if you are already a licensed attorney in one state, the path to practice law in another state can be arduous and fraught with ostensibly frivolous or inequitable barriers. In an age that prides itself on advances in mobility, there is something presumably askew about the state-by-state licensing differences and the erratic or idiosyncratic nature of the state-specific attorney admissions rules.

This is more than just mere annoyance since there are sharp teeth associated with getting caught practicing law unlawfully, even while a standing lawyer elsewhere, getting nabbed red-handed within a state that you are not properly authorized to perform legal tasks.

Looming over the heads of any such transgressors is the Unauthorized Practice of Law (UPL) provisions that carry stiff penalties and can turn things into the criminal realm for lawyers that cross a bridge too far on the matter.

The acrimonious discourse divides into three main camps:

- Open borders
- Strict borders
- Permeable borders

The open borders camp asserts that the law is the law.

This implies that if you are a practicing lawyer in one state then you ought to be free to practice law in another state. Geographic borders are an archaic relic from bygone days. In today's world, lawyers can easily go from state-to-state via modern-day transportation and not resort to horse and buggy. Furthermore, the use of remote or online lawyering is readily feasible via the Internet and advances in electronic networks. The border between one state and another one is merely a line on a map and makes no sense anymore as a stiff arm that prevents lawyers from doing their work wherever an Internet connection can be had.

Some proponents of the open borders approach would fervently assert that the different state requirements are now nothing more than a turf protection scheme that has outlived its time and creates a false and outmoded barrier-to-entry.

Those are fighting words, for sure, and can get the strict borders camp into a frenzy.

The strict borders viewpoint is that it makes abundant sense for each state to decide how it wants to set the requirements to practice law in their jurisdiction. We do indeed still live in a federated system that recognizes the sovereignty of the states. Furthermore, each state has its proprietary laws that apply to that state, which means that just because a lawyer from state X might know what they are doing in state X, they could readily be unaware of and out-of-touch with the laws of state Y.

To ensure that justice is being appropriately served, and to protect the public at large within a given state, the best and most exalted approach involves putting in place satisfactory requirements to uphold state-by-state particulars.

Case closed.

Those within the permeable borders camp are somewhere in-between the open borders versus strict borders extremists.

They beseech that a balanced measure of sensibility ought to be applied. There should be a ready form of reciprocity that is even-handed and streamlined. Keep any barriers or hurdles to a bare minimum. Give attorneys the benefit of the doubt in terms of being able to recast their legal beagle acumen in one state into another state. Let's get rid of the exasperating fragmented way of setting these requirements and have a harmonious standard that not only allows multidirectional efforts but also goes further to encourage and spark such mobility.

One would think that in an era of AI-based state-of-the-art mobility options such as the emergence of self-driving cars, there should be a path toward a multijurisdictional practice of law that befits contemporary times.

Speaking of AI, perhaps the infusion of AI into the legal profession and the practice of law will enter into this multijurisdictional calculus, as it were.

How so?

Predictions are that AI will increasingly become part of the burgeoning arena of LegalTech. Eventually, and some indicate inevitably, AI will become a vital armchair aid for conducting legal reasoning. There is even the possibility that AI will be crafted to autonomously undertake legal reasoning, providing AI capabilities to not merely support human lawyers but be able to undertake legal tasks directly, absent of human attorney intervention or supervision.

If or when that day arrives, the multijurisdictional question takes on a different aura, raising these matters:

- Should AI systems that are viably able to undertake legal reasoning be able to do so across states and within any state?

- Would each state simply require that the same admissions rules to practice law be applied to these AI systems as already occur for human attorneys?

- Might state-by-state requirements crumble when fully online and always available 24x7 AI-based legal reasoning systems become a norm in our society?

Keep in mind that AI legal reasoning is not some monolith wherein suddenly such systems are somehow all-knowing about the law across all states and all domains. The likelier scenario is that the AI is going to be crafted incrementally.

An entrepreneur or researcher might devise an AI legal reasoning system that handles the laws of say New York, but that same AI is utterly bereft of any legal acumen about California or any other state or territory. Akin to the simpler problem of handling sales tax issues from state-to-state (something that used to be problematic for programming in computers), AI legal reasoning systems are bound to be initially developed on a state-at-a-time basis.

Envision that an AI legal reasoning system would have state-by-state add-on modules. You might be doing work in Nevada, and begin to realize that you also need to perform some legal tasks in Hawaii, so you look online to find an available add-on AI pack that is certified for use in the Aloha State. By making use of that supplemental component, you might be then fully authorized to conduct legal tasks virtually there, never having set an actual foot on the picturesque beaches of the Hawaiian islands.

Conclusion

AI would appear to be the final straw on the camel's back about multijurisdictional discrepancies, though, then again, AI might be the solver that enables state-by-state idiosyncratic admission rules to remain and simply swallows them whole, as in the fashionable notion that software eats the world.

———————

Note: *For supplemental materials depicting the aspects discussed in this chapter, refer to Appendix B, which contains various augmented diagrams, charts, and additional related facets of relevance.*

CHAPTER 11

AI & LAW:

DIGITAL TWIN OF THE CONSTITUTION

Key briefing points about this article:

- Many assert that the United States Constitution is a living document

- Acrimonious debates occur over what the meaning of this "living" document ought to be

- Numerous camps have evolved about how to properly interpret the Constitution

- In modern times there are digital twins being developed for all kinds of entities

- It is useful to consider crafting an AI-based digital twin of the Constitution

Introduction

There is little doubt that the United States Constitution is an amazing document and provides a stellar example of how mankind can devise laws that seek to balance governmental powers and the fundamental rights of the people.

Imagine what might have happened if the Constitution had not been crafted. One can only shudder at where we might be today.

Suppose that the Constitution had indeed been crafted but that it was worded differently than what was finally composed. Where would we be? Some might argue that we could very well be in the same status of still trying to figure out what the framers intended versus what their words seem to state. Overall, the words used in the finalized version are still merely words, suggesting that they are open to interpretation and provide viably alternative meaning.

That's partially why some refer to the cherished document as the living Constitution.

Please give deep thought to the use of the word "living" in this context. Many legal scholars and even the everyday public say that the U.S. Constitution is a living document, but few if any would argue that it can actually breathe on its own or take a step as a living animal might do. Unless you are off your rocker, the notion of living herein is not something that is sentient and instead proffers the connotations of a written sentiment that is malleable and interpretably changeable over time.

How far though can one, or should one, bend this statuesque marker?

Some are quick to point out that the developers of the Constitution did not have rocket ships that could get to the moon and nor did they have jet planes to fly them around the emerging nation. In that sense, when they wrote and ratified the Constitution, there was much unknown to them about the future. This logically leads to the assertion that the words of the Constitution should be viewed as a framework or template since it could not have anticipated the myriad of societal changes that would subsequently arise.

There are those that lament that by caving in and agreeing that the Constitution is merely a framework, you open a Pandora's box of bad tidings. An ominous slippery slope is started.

One way or another, we will inadvertently slide our way into ever more distancing interpretations of what the framers intended. Think of the famous example of whispering into one person's ear in a long line of people, each of which attempts to whisper the same message to the next in line, and inevitably at the end you have a message that no longer resembles the original one. An inherent danger awaits us as we seemingly cast and recast the Constitution over time, ultimately usurping the wisdom embodied in the venerated document, some so exhort.

President Woodrow Wilson in 1908 had stated that "living political constitutions must be Darwinian in structure and in practice" (indicated in his esteemed treatise on the *Constitutional Government in the United States*). Perhaps all constitutions, no matter when written and regardless of how carefully composed, would forever be insufficient as a means of codifying the law. Mankind is bound by the laws of nature and thus a document establishing the rule of law will always be subject to nature's ways, including the need to adapt for survival's sake.

The framers were not blind to the likelihood of their work being reinterpreted and recast. Historians point out that there was much debate about how to try and word the Constitution. The hope was to use relatively precise language and seek to avoid overly wild or far-reaching offshoots that would no longer resemble what they had in mind.

Of course, language is a dicey thing that intrinsically is semantically indeterminate. Trying to be ironclad by the words that you use is somewhat futile as there is indubitably alternative meaning that can be derived.

Numerous camps exist for how to appropriately interpret the Constitution.

One of the most well-known is the originalists. Generally, without drawing ire for being overly succinct herein, the notion of originalism entails staying as close as possible to the original meaning of the Constitution.

This could be based on what the framers had in mind. This could also be based on what the people at large had as an understanding of what the document stated.

As an example of the thorny debate about what originalism constitutes, consider these remarks that Supreme Court Justice Scalia gave in his 1996 speech detailing his viewpoint of constitutional interpretation:

> "The theory of originalism treats a constitution like a statute, and gives it the meaning that its words were understood to bear at the time they were promulgated. You will sometimes hear it described as the theory of original intent. You will never hear me refer to original intent, because as I say I am first of all a textualist, and secondly an originalist. If you are a textualist, you don't care about the intent, and I don't care if the framers of the Constitution had some secret meaning in mind when they adopted its words. I take the words as they were promulgated to the people of the United States, and what is the fairly understood meaning of those words."

In short, there are ongoing debates about the meaning of the Constitution, including and especially acrimonious debates about how we ought to be deriving that meaning.

Let's shift gears and consider two newer avenues that might help these debates. One realm of more recent note is the emergence of so-called digital twins. The other arena consists of advances in Artificial Intelligence (AI).

Digital Twins And AI Usage

A digital twin is considered to be a digitally based replica of an entity.

The entity can be a non-living contraption such as an airplane engine or a turbine, or it can be a living being.

Digital twins were initially conceived as a means to aid in the manufacturing and deployment of complex machinery.

If you were going to make an aircraft engine, it made sense to first craft a computer-based simulation to ascertain whether the engine will work. Furthermore, once the aircraft engine is manufactured, you can use its digital twin to try and ascertain why the engine might be faltering while in the field.

Digital twins are getting increasingly sophisticated via the advent of AI being infused into the digital twin capabilities.

Here's then the idea to ruminate on:

> *Should we embark upon an AI-enabled digital twin of the United States Constitution?*

The idea is being bandied around and provides the possibility of turning the non-living "living" Constitution into something that would ostensibly be enlivened by being actively responsive and altogether quite useful for judicial efforts.

Conclusion

Do not though assume that this will remove us from the morass about the meaning of the Constitution. In some ways, it could illuminate the meaning, whilst in other ways, it might spark added contentions.

Maybe best to keep your eyes wide open and be on the watch for that AI-based digital twin, and ponder what John Adams, Thomas Jefferson, James Madison, and the rest of the crew would have thought about such modern-day mechanizations of their prized work.

Note: *For supplemental materials depicting the aspects discussed in this chapter, refer to Appendix B, which contains various augmented diagrams, charts, and additional related facets of relevance.*

CHAPTER 12

AI & LAW:

ANTITRUST AND AI (AAI)

Key briefing points about this essay:

- Antitrust law has once again been brought to the forefront of society

- A recent spate of antitrust lawsuits against tech firms catches the eye and worldwide attention

- We need to be cautious in overstepping our instant assumption that antitrust has occurred

- To aid in the antitrust vigilance proposition we can adopt the use of AI for antitrust endeavors

- Via the use of AI-based antitrust diligence systems, the vigilance can be notably enhanced

Introduction

It seems that the daily news is filled with breathtaking stories about antitrust violations, or at least alleged such violations.

Of course, we have to remain diligent and await the outcome of these antitrust lawsuits before we can summarily slam the targeted firms. Antitrust is a complex case to be made and there are abundant chances that the allegations will end-up falling apart.

Give the accused their day in court, one might implore. Yet, despite that sage advice, there is a strong temptation to look at the accused firms and believe that one readily spies what appears to be clear-and-present indications of antitrust practices. Anyway, allow the gears of justice to work their grinding mechanizations and then we will presumably know.

One of the latest headlines entails an antitrust lawsuit filed by nearly forty states that have accused Google of exercising monopolistic power over the online search marketplace. The suit alleges that this vaunted Alphabet Incorporated entity carried out a scheme involving anticompetitive practices, doing so in the outright and flagrant conduct of its business activities and in the contracts that it has insidiously put in place. Meanwhile, Google denies that any such antitrust violations have occurred, explaining that their business efforts and allure to consumers showcase that their online search predominance is highly competitive and proffers the best in product design and technological capability.

The one solace for Google is that they are not the only recent headline-making antitrust-accused tech firm since there have been similar newsworthy antitrust qualms leveled at Facebook and others.

Of course, that's an antitrust-alleged sacred group or special club that few would wish to be a member of. About the only thing we can say for sure is that these antitrust allegations and investigations are likely to play out over a lengthy period, and there are bound to be splintering offshoots that will surface along this quite rocky and painstakingly arduous antitrust-assessing journey.

For anyone interested in particularly excellent research on antitrust in today's tech spurred world, I highly recommend the work by esteemed colleague Professor Thibault Schrepel at the Utrecht University School of Law (he also serves at the University of Paris, and as a faculty associate at Harvard, plus a CodeX Fellow at Stanford University).

In one of his papers published this year in the *NYU Journal of Law & Liberty*, he propounds that antitrust laws must not become romanticized and used to pit the tech elites versus the public at large: "Increasing romanticization could critically jeopardize decades of jurisprudential construction, causing economic disruption, destabilization of the law, and blindness towards real anti-competitive practices on the part of antitrust authorities, consequently placing the rule of law at risk."

Schrepel mentions this growing concern as a general cautionary wake-up call and not as a direct commentary on these latest headline-grabbing instances. Whether this newest spate of antitrust allegations is a byproduct of the current political climate and polarization, or whether they are straight ahead and unequivocally undeniable instances of antitrust is a matter yet to be ascertained.

You might also relish his paper entitled "Predatory Innovation: The Definite Need for Legal Recognition" that appeared in the *SMU Science and Technology Law Review* in 2018. In this cornerstone piece, he defines and proffers that we need to encapsulate predatory innovation into the vernacular of antitrust law:

"In fact, the terms of *predatory innovation*—which the author defines as the alteration of one or more technical elements of a product to limit or eliminate competition—describes all practices that, under the guise of real innovations, are anti-competitive strategies aimed at eliminating competition without benefiting consumers."

This emphasis is especially poignant and strikes prophetically at the heart of the current suit against Google since a crucial element that underpins the allegations involves Google having implemented new features into its search engine that can be judged as either cast for purely competitive reasons (their presumed assertion) or undertaken by employing a monopolistic practice to freeze out their competitors.

AI As An Aid To Antitrust Vigilance

Shifting gears, the topic of antitrust also raises another interesting facet about the future of the law, namely the gradual adoption of Artificial Intelligence (AI) into the law and the leveraging of autonomous legal reasoning systems.

How will AI be instrumental and integrated into antitrust modernizations?

I've indicated that the use of AI will be infused into the entire lifecycle of antitrust undertakings.

For each of the stages or phases of an antitrust effort, you can expect that AI will be imbued into the activities and will at times aid the lawyers and human-conducted efforts and will at other times be working autonomously to grind through antitrust pursuits. Based on the U.S. Department of Justice (DOJ) *Antitrust Division Manual*, there is ample opportunity for AI and computer-based smart systems to substantively enhance today's principally manually laden and paper-pushing antitrust investigative procedures and case development processes.

My framework defines the antitrust lifecycle as consisting of six major stages or phases, and for which AI will become a vital collaborator in all crucial respects:

1) **Detection** – seeking to identify potential antitrust violations
2) **Assessment** – ascertaining if there is a civil or criminal case of prosecutorial merit
3) **Investigation** – establishing (or not) the case to support an asserted antitrust violation

4) **Recommendation** – indicating whether a formal civil or criminal suit should be launched
5) **Prosecuting** -- aiding or carrying out the antitrust case in our courts
6) **Implementation** – undertaking the required judgment monitoring and enforcement

Briefly, consider for example the first stage that entails the detection of a potential antitrust violation.

This first-step aspect of detection or discovery is a lot harder to achieve than a cursory glance might so suggest. The AI would use Natural Language Processing (NLP) capabilities to analyze complaints lodged by consumers and businesses that claim antitrust conduct is taking place in the marketplace. Customized NLP would also be continually assessing media reports about antitrust potentialities. Furthermore, information from government informants that have applied for leniency under the antitrust leniency programs would be examined, and so would the formal complaints filed by U.S. Attorneys and by the states. Etc.

This is a voluminous amount of data that by-hand is overwhelming to keep up with. Sophisticated AI techniques combined with the NLP, such as the latest in Machine Learning and Deep Learning, would be able to computationally continually be scanning and assessing such material. In a likewise fashion, each of the other stages of the antitrust process can be advanced via the use of AI. AI for antitrust provides scalability and would inure a greater use of data-based metrics and transparency in antitrust vigilance.

Conclusion

Though you might assume that the AI would also resolve and prevent the occurrence of politically motivated antitrust accusations, do not be so sure about that presumptive thought. Those that adapt and shape the AI can still force their imprint upon what the AI will be doing.

As a final comment, the Federal Trade Commission (FTC) refers to the DOJ Antitrust Division as *The Enforcers* of the antitrust laws. AI can become a companion enforcer, albeit the word "enforcer" in this context certainly seems ominous and reminiscent of those sci-fi world-dominance scenarios. Maybe we should refer to the AI for antitrust vigilance as *The Protector* or perhaps *The Guardian* (well, those could be equally disquieting, one supposes).

.

Note: *For supplemental materials depicting the aspects discussed in this chapter, refer to Appendix B, which contains various augmented diagrams, charts, and additional related facets of relevance.*

CHAPTER 13

AI & LAW:

AI ARBITRATOR IMPARTIALITY ISSUES

Key briefing points about this article:

- Arbitration consists of one or more arbitrators and the associated parties to the case

- A party might accuse an arbitrator of having biases that impacted impartiality

- Disclosure pre-case is intended to aid in avoiding selecting a potentially biased arbitrator

- Futurists of the law are anticipating that AI will have a notable role in arbitrations

- Turns out it is a commonly accepted false assumption that the AI will be bereft of biases

Introduction

Arbitrators are often greeted with delight at the beginning of a case and then treated with disdain after the arbitration has been decided, especially by any party that feels they were somehow gypped or got a raw deal.

One minute the arbitrator is the superhero for taking the case, the next they are the grimy goat for having bungled how the arbitration proceeded and the result produced.

The odds are that however an arbitrator will end-up ruling on a case, one of the parties is going to be upset and undoubtedly disgruntled with the ruling. Besides the obvious avenue of trying to contest the arbitrator's actual decision, there is the possibility of undercutting the arbitrator by a claim of undue bias or some form of partiality that was detrimental to your case.

There is an entire focus of research regarding the role of arbitrator biases and the notion of impartiality.

Some liken this line of legal reasoning as similar to going after a referee about an alleged bad call during a baseball or football game. Of course, that analogy breaks down somewhat since you might argue that an arbitrator is not the same as a referee (having different duties and obligations), plus the ability to overturn a sporting match is not quite in the same league as trying to overturn the outcome of an arbitration.

In any case, where there is a will, there is a way, and as such those that are dissatisfied with an arbitrator's decision will seek to blemish the arbitrator if this seems a viable means of challenging the result. And, for clarification, it certainly could be the case that the arbitrator embodied a bias and exhibited either implicitly or explicitly said biases in a manner that was unduly impactful to the handling of the arbitration and the end-result produced.

Starkly stated, an arbitrator could have been biased. The bias could have impacted the process and could have impacted the decision. On the same token, the bias could have averted materially impacting the process, though it could have impacted the decision. Yet another variation is that the bias could have averted impacting the process and nor impacted the decision, yet nonetheless, there was still a taint of bias throughout (but, if it had no impact, this certainly diminishes the bias wielding foil).

The other possibility is that the arbitrator had no material bias at all. In which case, there can still be an attempt to impute bias, taking us back to the aforementioned avenues of challenging the arbitration.

Professor William Park proffered this memorable quote in his Boston University School of Law research paper on the contentious topic of arbitrator bias:

"From the command post of bland generalities, the job of evaluating independence or impartiality may seem simple. In light of specific challenges, however, the task becomes one of nuance and complexity, often implicating subtle wrinkles to the comportment of otherwise honorable and experienced individuals" (2015, Legal Theory Paper No. 15-39).

There is an expectation that arbitrators will reveal beforehand any potential disclosures that could somehow impact a potential arbitration case, and thus allow the parties to seek another arbitrator in lieu of the one being considered. Attempts to contest an arbitrator are often done post-case on a claim that the arbitrator failed to pre-case disclose their past, though the courts have generally tried to establish a balancing act on this angle of attack.

As pointed out in a salient *Daily Journal* column by Michael Leb on December 23, 2020, the California Supreme Court has stated:

"The arbitrator cannot reasonably be expected to identify and disclose all events in the arbitrator's past, including those not connected to the parties, the facts, or the issues in controversy, that conceivably might cause a party to prefer another arbitrator" (*Haworth v Superior Court*, 2010).

If the arbitrator made sufficient disclosures beforehand, and a later complaining party argues after-the-fact that the arbitrator had a bias going into the case, the road is a tough one to hoe since the counterargument is that you knew and accepted the already stated sustenance of the arbitrator else you would have presumably sought a different arbitrator at the start.

Of course, there is still a chance of claiming that it was not clear that the bias would enter into your particular case, or that it entered surprisingly in a vile way that was unexpected, and so on.

We can go round and round on the myriad of ways to lobe accusations of arbitrator bias or partiality that one asserts led to an unfair or unbalanced decision.

AI and the Future of Arbitration

Shifting gears, there are rising hopes that the use of Artificial Intelligence (AI) will gradually become a meaningful addition to the pursuit of arbitration.

The idea is that an AI system devised specifically for performing arbitration might be utilized by human arbitrators, doing so to provide guidance and assistance during the arbitration process.

This includes the use of Natural Language Processing (NLP) so that the arbitrator and the parties can somewhat converse in normal speech and writing, and the AI will be able to keep up with any discourse during the arbitration.

There would also be the use of Machine Learning and Deep Learning, which are AI approaches entailing computational pattern matching, enabling the case to be compared to a vast corpus of other prior arbitrations and ergo proffer predictions or insights accordingly thereof.

Inevitably, it is assumed that someday the AI will be able to autonomously reason and there might not be a need for a human arbitrator in some arbitration cases.

Now for the rub.

Some seem to think that having AI as an arbitrator would be a kind of godsend since it would presumably dispense with any further concerns over biases in arbitration. The AI is portrayed as perfectly impartial.

Sorry to burst that bubble, but the truth of the matter is that the AI could assuredly be imbued with biases. We are already beginning to witness the widespread problems of AI systems that have embedded biases, and this trend is going to continue, sadly so.

The biases are sometimes carried into the AI by the developers, while in other instances the AI "learns" the biases over time via the ongoing use of Machine Learning and Deep Learning efforts.

Conclusion

The bad news is that AI-based arbitrators are not going to be bereft entirely of bias.

The goods news, if you wish to call it that, will be that the possibility of gaining a challenge over an arbitration will remain an open option, even in a world of AI-run and AI deciding arbitrations, albeit you'll likely need some sharp AI specialists and Data Scientists to provide the needed indications of intrinsic bias.

What did the AI know, and when did it know, will become a common refrain in that era.

Note: *For supplemental materials depicting the aspects discussed in this chapter, refer to Appendix B, which contains various augmented diagrams, charts, and additional related facets of relevance.*

CHAPTER 14

AI & LAW:
THINK FAST AND THINK SLOW

Key briefing points about this essay:

- A popular metacognition model is that humans have a twofold approach to how our minds work

- One portion of our minds thinks fast, making snap decisions, called *System 1* (M-consciousness)

- The other portion thinks slow, analytically so, and is known as *System 2* (I-consciousness)

- This viewpoint about the mind can be applied to lawyers and performing legal reasoning

- AI has likewise the sub-symbolics and the symbolics camps

Introduction

The yin and the yang.

Thinking fast and thinking slow.

What's this fuss all about?

There is an ongoing assertion that the human mind is composed of two divisible forms of cognition, characterized as consisting of the fast-thinking realm and its conjoined twin the slow-thinking domain.

The fast-thinking portion allows us to make snap decisions. It is said to be the part of your brain that kicks into gear for making rapid and intuitive style decisions, often labeled as gut instinct, and more formally referred to simply as *System 1* (a rather stark naming, for sure, with catchier names having been floated such as the M-consciousness wherein the letter M stands for mysterious).

Meanwhile, there is the slow-thinking portion that proffers the logic-based part of human decision making. This contains a decidedly deliberative capacity that allows us to perform analytic style endeavors. Whereas fast-thinking seems to skip past the arduous effort of being step-by-step mindful, the slow-thinking portion takes its sweet time and figures out things via an amalgamation of cognitive heavy lifting. The slow-thinking element is commonly known as *System 2* and carries an alternative moniker with a bit more pizzazz, the so-called information infused mental engine or I-consciousness.

Nobel Prize winner in Economics, Daniel Kahneman, wrote and published a quite popular book covering this two-for-one theory of the mind, doing so in 2011 with his "Thinking, Fast and Slow" compendium. His discussion stoked an already percolating belief in this dividing of cognition propositional conjecture, and since then there has been a persistent interest for those trying to prove or perhaps disprove this acclaimed assertion about our minds.

There are numerous caveats associated with this whole concoction of how the mind works, along with angst that this is an exceedingly narrow way to conceive of the mind and perhaps leads us inadvertently down a dead-end or at least somewhat wasteful path toward understanding the human mind.

One of the most vocalized concerns is that the theory smacks of being a stark dichotomy about cognition, as though there are only two modes and nothing more. We might be waylaid by fixating on the alleged two modes, missing the boat as we completely ignore or disregard that there might be three, four, five, or some greater number of more sensible and appropriate ways to carve up cognitive facilities.

Another qualm is the base assumption entailing the contention that fast-thinking is fast and that slow-thinking is slow (well, yes, this is indeed an exceedingly apparent, self-evidentiary claim underlying the core concept). First, the relative timing difference might be of a negligible degree and ergo egregiously mischaracterizes mental exertions in a rather clunky and inappropriate manner. Second, there would seem to be indications that the fast-thinking can at times be slower than the slow-thinking, commensurate with the slow-thinking potentially being faster than the fast-thinking.

All told, those that stridently focus on metacognition, essentially the discipline or schooling of thinking about how we think, do not all agree with the *System 1* and *System 2* propositional notions. If you want to have some fun, albeit with sparks to fly, here's a small joke or needling that you can play on such believers.

What gets their goat is when some suggest that 95% of your average day consists of the fast-thinking taking place, while the remaining 5% of your day is the slow-thinking. This mythical rule-of-thumb seems to be repeated over and over again, having an appealing ring to it and insidiously feels satisfying, yet there is insufficient bona fide evidence to support such a bold contention and altogether is cast as woefully misleading and inelegantly misused.

Suppose though that we voluntarily agree to give due consideration to the fast-thinking and slow-thinking model of the human mind and see what it can do for us. Despite any misgivings or nagging qualms, let's try out this popular metacognition vehicle and take it for a spin.

Lawyers And The Twofold Way Of Thinking

Lawyers are presumably subject to the *System 1* and *System 2* forms of thinking since they are by definition humans and therefore embody this dichotomous form of cognition. When standing in front of a judge and arguing a case, the odds are that you've done a lot of prep beforehand and have lined up a slew of carefully composed logic-based arguments. All of a sudden, the judge stops you midsentence and asks a tough and unexpected question.

What happens inside your brain?

The *System 1* or fast-thinking portion comes up with an off-the-cuff answer and you utter some words to quickly showcase that you are being responsive to the judge. At the same time, your *System 2* or slow-thinking portion is attempting feverishly to piece together an analytical answer. The utterance of words from your *System 1* snap thinking is buying time for *System 2* to get its act together and come up with something more substantive.

Briefly, some attorneys get jammed-up because they are weak in *System 1*, the fast-thinking, and stronger in System 2, slow-thinking. This means that there can be a seemingly long pause there in court as you are attempting to use the slow-thinking portion, and are unable to do those quick quips. Without the rapid capacity of thinking on your feet, this provides an opening for the opposing attorney to jump into the fray and make it seem as though you are stumped. The judge might equally get an impression that you have no answer and have been snagged by a gotcha or gaping hole in your case.

Of course, the other side of that coin can be bad too. If your fast-thinking blurts out just anything at all, it can pin you into a posture that your slow-thinking would have never led you.

Shifting gears, consider how Artificial Intelligence (AI) will be added into this mix.

The use of AI for legal reasoning is going to increasingly be apparent in our courts and all facets of the law.

Within the AI field, some assert the true path to AI is going to be via the use of Machine Learning and Deep Learning, which are approaches that utilize computational pattern matching and are considered in the sub-symbolics camp of AI development.

Meanwhile, others in AI tout the logic-based approaches, perhaps you might recall the days of Expert Systems and Knowledge-based Systems, for which these are called the symbolics camp of AI development.

The sub-symbolics are akin to System 1 of thinking, while the symbolics is aiming toward System 2 of human thought.

This highlights the added assertion that perhaps both are needed to achieve AI, working in a conjoined manner.

Or it could be that once again we've fallen into a false dichotomy and maybe there are more and better ways to pursue AI achievement.

Conclusion

I'd ask you to decide about the twofold model of cognition by indicating whether you agree or disagree with it, but that seems like yet another dichotomous way to shape the world, and do not want to fall into a mental trap about it, so let's give our combined fast-thinking and slow-thinking ample time to figure this all out).

.

Note: *For supplemental materials depicting the aspects discussed in this chapter, refer to Appendix B, which contains various augmented diagrams, charts, and additional related facets of relevance.*

CHAPTER 15

AI & LAW:
LEGAL PERSONHOOD

Key briefing points about this essay:

- One means of applying the law to AI consists of considering how to best legally govern AI

- There are ongoing debates about whether AI should or should not have legal personhood

- Sometimes an argument is aided by looking at extremes

- An extreme viewpoint of today's AI is the notion of a future kind of AI known as spontaneous

- Discussion of a spontaneous form of AI gives new potential insights for the governance of AI

Introduction

Whenever considering how AI and the law come together, it is useful to consider these two major paths: (1) applying AI to the law, and (2) applying the law to AI. There is no particular sequence or priority of the two paths. They are equally fruitful and of equal import.

Let's herein tackle the application of AI to the law, and then come around to the application of the law to AI.

The crux of applying AI to the law is readily seen via AI that is increasingly being included in LegalTech, thusly expanding and easing the use of computer-based systems for legal professionals. Consider for example the ongoing efforts to leverage Natural Language Processing (NLP) capabilities to semantically examine legal documents and attempt to render legally minded interpretations, plus the use of Machine Learning to computationally undertake extensive pattern matching and make judicial-oriented predictions about court cases, and so on. These are all ostensibly considered various means by which AI can be applied to the law.

The other approach, considered the other side of this two-sided coin, involves applying the law to AI.

Generally, this alternative way of mixing the law and AI consists of confronting governance issues involving the emergence and advent of semi-intelligence and ultimately fully intelligent computing. The assumption is that the intelligent-like behaviors that can arise via AI are going to spur a need to reconsider and possibly revamp the law when it comes to legal personhood.

It is said that we will inevitably and inextricably find ourselves having to grapple with the reality that an artificial system will verge upon attributes that we normally associate only with human intelligence. If that day comes, a thorny question arises as to whether we would merely reapply the existing laws about personhood and declare that they equally apply to AI, or we might ascertain that some kind of special and newly minted laws might be needed to encompass this other form of intelligent behavior.

Some decry that this idea or belief that we would equate human-based legal personhood with a form of AI-based systems is utterly ridiculous and akin to mindlessly reading too many sci-fic wild-eyed tales.

Those critics are apt to point out that we do not yet today have any semblance of AI that is sentient, not even close to that vaunted goal, and therefore this talk of personhood is absurdly premature, perhaps like the boy that cried wolf and amounts to much ado about nothing.

The counterargument is that just because we are not yet at the point of sentience, this does not mean we ought to have our heads dug deeply into the sand and be pretending that such a day will not arrive. As is well-taught in scouting, and presumably at the heart of being a keen lawyer, we always need to be prepared. Better to be safe than sorry and avert finding ourselves behind the eight ball because we waited until the genie was out of the bottle to figure out what laws will apply to this extraordinary form of intelligence.

Shifting Gears Into Spontaneous AI

Whenever you want to carry on an argument to any lengthy degree, sometimes a handy way to do so involves stretching the argument to its extremes. Doing so will possibly reveal new revelations that otherwise less open-ended argumentation on a topic did not particularly uncover.

This brings us to an interesting research paper that speculates about a variant of AI that the authors imaginatively depict as being a spontaneous version of traditional AI, which they name as SI (Spontaneous Intelligence). The research was undertaken by Jiahong Chen, School of Law, University of Edinburgh, and Paul Burgess, Faculty of Laws, University College of London, in their paper entitled "The Boundaries of Legal Personhood: How Spontaneous Intelligence can Problematise Differences Between Humans, Artificial Intelligence, Companies and Animals" (published in *Artificial Intelligence and Law*, September 28, 2018).

In brief, traditional AI is the type of AI that we are currently seeing come to fruition in our everyday world, such as the NLP used by Siri and Alexa, or the AI that is being used for self-driving cars.

You might find of tangential but relevant interest that there is a brouhaha brewing about the responsible party when a self-driving car gets into a car crash. Do you hold the AI driving system responsible, as though it has personhood facilities, or do you assign fault instead to the human wizards that put the system in place?

Per this research paper about personhood, the authors assert that today's AI driving systems do not rate personhood, and we instead need to focus on the human overlords (in my lingo, as it were): "There must, in accordance with the mores of modern society, be some way to attribute blame somewhere for this sort of action. In common with the issues outlined above in relation to an SI and legal sanctions, it would seem peculiar to try to sanction the car itself, but there could be a sheeting home of a bundle of liabilities to multiple stakeholders. Those include the owners of the vehicle, the developer of the software, the manufacturer of the components, or even the provider of information."

So what is this other variant of AI, the SI, and its nature, and how might it differ in a legal personhood sensibility?

Imagine that an AI evolves on its own, across the vast worldwide Internet, and becomes pervasive and ubiquitous, giving rise to an unprecedented spontaneous form of artificial intelligence. The authors suggest this: "In these terms, we consider the challenges that may arise where SI as an entity: has no owner, no designer, and no controller; has evolved into existence as a non-human created intelligence; is autonomous; has no physical form; and, although it exists around the world, exists in no particular jurisdiction."

You can't pin the tail on the donkey on any specific human that would hold direct and irrefutable responsibility for the SI.

The research concludes that this envisioned SI is more akin to humans and the potential ascribing of personhood, than is traditional AI and personhood, offering this somewhat surprising result: "We have come to a somewhat counter-intuitive conclusion: an SI actually shares more characteristics in common with humans than AI.

This is not to say an SI is necessarily similar to humans; we are merely illuminating the relational position that an SI shares more in common with humans than humans share with AI."

Conclusion

At least one thing is hopefully abundantly clear, not all AI is the same, and there are significant reasons to reimagine today's laws as it relates to personhood, especially since the rule-of-thumb that one size does *not* fit all is worthy of rapt legal attention.

.

———

Note: *For supplemental materials depicting the aspects discussed in this chapter, refer to Appendix B, which contains various augmented diagrams, charts, and additional related facets of relevance.*

CHAPTER 16

AI & LAW:
LOWER COURTS AND AI JUDGES

Key briefing points about this essay:

- There is much debate about the possibility of AI serving as judges in our courts

- Some argue it should never be permitted, others say it will be inevitable and unstoppable

- One argument being made is that perhaps AI judges would be solely used in the lower courts

- The logic for use at the lower courts includes scalability and consistency

- Countering points are that this drains humanity from the lower courts and is a slippery slope

Introduction

Do you lay awake at night due to the notion that someday we will have AI-based autonomous judges in our courtrooms, looming over humanity and deciding the fate of humans that come before their grand majesty?

So that you don't needlessly lose an excess of sleep, please be aware that this kind of AI is still only a gleam in the eye of AI developers. A long and bumpy road has to be first crossed to get there. That being said, it is important to realize there is semi-autonomous AI that might reach that goal line sooner than we think.

In the case of AI that is semi-autonomous and likely to be nothing more than a supplemental aid to a human judge, there is little argument that such high-tech would be a handy sidekick. Perhaps such AI could tidy up the loose ends of any legal arguments or provide insights about precedents via being able to readily peruse thousands upon thousands of prior cases. Generally, there is minimal controversy associated with arming the judiciary with so-called "smart" computer-based systems that serve at the will of human judges and can ostensibly bolster adjudication toward greater efficiencies.

The real war of words arises when you start thinking about fully autonomous AI that imbues legal reasoning and can seemingly render judicial decisions without the need for human hands or minds. That type of AI would not be supplemental and instead would outright replace human judges (this is not to suggest that there would only be AI-based judges, as there might be a mixture of sometimes the use of a human judge and in other instances the use of an AI one).

The shorthand version of the spirited controversy is whether we should allow AI on its own to serve in *any* such judicial capacity.

Some argue that there will never be a viable means for this AI autonomy to be utilized, even if it can be crafted (none of this heightened AI yet exists).

Others take a decidedly opposite tack and emphasize that we could use AI across all levels of the courts and in any and all judging roles. Assuming that AI can be established to provide the equivalent of what human judges do, the hope by proponents of this kind of technology would be to use it broadly and deeply throughout our courts.

Another viewpoint is that maybe these autonomous AI judges should be confined to a particular focus or segment of our courts. At the International Bar Association (IBA) annual conference in November 2020, Dean Tania Sourdin of Australia's Newcastle University Law School remarked that the lower courts might be the appropriate setting: "'It seems to me that judges at lower court levels are likely to be phased out" (see *The Law Society Gazette*, November 9, 2020 article entitled "IBA 2020: Robots Don Black Cap For Lower Court Judges).

This lower court infusion of AI-based autonomous judges might not necessarily apply across-the-board entailing all areas of the law. Professor Sourdin indicated that family law and various aspects of criminal law are likely carveouts. Legal avenues that seem particularly amenable would be "the simple civil cases, possibly personal injury cases, and certainly very simple contractual matters," according to Sourdin.

Okay, for sake of argument, let's take at face value the plausibility of using AI-based autonomous judges in the lower courts. Meanwhile, agree too that such AI judges won't be used at the appeals courts and thus intentionally *not* applied in the higher courts.

What might be the line of argumentation that supports this angle or slice of mechanization and what might be the counterarguments?

Going Toe-to-Toe On The Lower Courts

We'll start with the foundation in favor of the AI autonomous judges as serving only at the lower courts level and thus distinctly not being used at the higher courts. Notice that there is no need to delve into the argument of not using such tech at all as judges since we are momentarily stipulating that we'll forego that qualm. Presumably, without undue bickering, let's assume that this kind of AI is going to be used somewhere in the courts, albeit in a narrower rather than an all-encompassing manner.

First, a popular supportive argument is that the use of AI at the lower courts would tremendously help in coping with the voluminous amount of court activity that occurs in the lower courts. There are ongoing calls that more judges are desperately needed, along with the decrying of justice potentially being delayed as a result of an insufficient number of qualified judges at the ready. AI-based autonomous judges could easily scale-up or scale-down, being on the go and always available for whatever need for judging might be at the lower courts (i.e., the AI provides the supply to always meet the demand).

Secondly, the AI would provide a semblance of consistency that is unachievable with the use of human judges. Human judges act not simply by the nature of the law, they also embody personal preferences and styles as permitted within the range of the law and the myriad of court procedures. There is also the point made that human judges are in fact human, meaning they are subject to human emotions and human foibles. Many assume that AI-based autonomous judges won't be (this is a contested topic since there are indeed real concerns about AI-related inherent biases).

Thirdly, by having human judges at the higher courts, we preserve our overall sense of the law and can assume and rely upon those human judges to be a backstop or failsafe. The assumption is that even if the AI goes astray, doing so on occasion at the lower courts, the human judges at the higher courts will catch these maladies and decisively rejuvenate justice accordingly.

Now, let's wade into the counterarguments.

For most citizens, their first contact with the judicial system arises at the lower courts. At that point of entry, assuming there are these widespread AI judges, the public at large is being handed over to a machine, as it were. Some eschew the lack of humanity that would be conveyed and the cold and calculated message that it would send.

Another concern is that the number of appeals might grow astronomically. The lower courts would simply become a spitfire feeder and overwhelm the higher courts.

And, for some the most frightening aspect is that the lower courts are nothing more than the start of a slippery slope. If this AI does a sufficient job at the lower courts, you can anticipate that the higher court days of human judges are sorely numbered.

Conclusion

For those of you that are pining away about these AI-based autonomous judges, the good news is that you've got time before this capability of AI emerges.

Meanwhile, do not be surprised to see the supportive style semi-autonomous AI that soon becomes the best pal of human judges, and be ready to make your case to a bench that has got a double-punch of both human and AI sitting there in judgment.

.

———

Note: *For supplemental materials depicting the aspects discussed in this chapter, refer to Appendix B, which contains various augmented diagrams, charts, and additional related facets of relevance.*

CHAPTER 17

AI & LAW:
REPRESENTATIONAL CONFLICTS

Key briefing points about this essay:

- Lawyers are to avoid conflicts of interest in the lawyer-client relationship

- It is hard to imagine one attorney vigorously representing two opposing clients

- The future of the law includes the infusion of AI-based legal reasoning systems

- We will ultimately have AI that can be the lawyer in the lawyer-client relationship

- Consider whether there are potential conflicts of interest by that AI representation

Introduction

We take at relatively face value that a lawyer representing a client is not simultaneously representing a client on the opposing side of the case at hand.

This would seem like a rather obvious conflict of interest.

The attorney would ostensibly be arguing against their own stated position, each of which are presumably diametrically opposed on some core elements of the case. Almost as though a cartoonish portrayal, envision the attorney rushing from side-to-side in a courtroom and pretending to be fervently trouncing the opponent, namely themself.

A quite odd spectacle and one unbefitting our adversarial form of justice.

It is a well-known and commonly accepted canon that the lawyer-client relationship has special properties, including the avoidance of potential conflicts of interest. As much as feasible, any conflicts of interest entailing a lawyer and their client are to be identified at the soonest possible appearance, or even upon the anticipation thereof, and either averted or otherwise sufficiently resolved properly.

The ABA provides this notable stipulation: "Loyalty and independent judgment are essential elements in the lawyer's relationship to a client. Concurrent conflicts of interest can arise from the lawyer's responsibilities to another client, a former client, or a third person or from the lawyer's own interests."

That seems like a rather self-evident credo.

The rationale for averting a conflict of interest is straightforward, per the ABA: "The client as to whom the representation is directly adverse is likely to feel betrayed, and the resulting damage to the client-lawyer relationship is likely to impair the lawyer's ability to represent the client effectively. In addition, the client on whose behalf the adverse representation is undertaken reasonably may fear that the lawyer will pursue that client's case less effectively out of deference to the other client, i.e., that the representation may be materially limited by the lawyer's interest in retaining the current client."

In our adversarial approach to adjudication, we certainly grasp the abundant and perhaps obvious logic in having two opposing attorneys that each is independently able to legally battle vigorously for their respective clients.

Imagine if one attorney represented both sides of a case, serving as the sole representation for clients that were opposing each other. This seems inherently a dicey notion. Can the lawyer adequately and forcefully represent both sides of a case? It is a doubtful proposition.

There are some exceptions allowed for varying kinds or degrees of conflict of interest, including that there is the possibility of permitting a conflict if the client agrees to the standing conflict, requiring therefore informed consent by the client (via the ABA): "Loyalty to a current client prohibits undertaking representation directly adverse to that client without that client's informed consent. Thus, absent consent, a lawyer may not act as an advocate in one matter against a person the lawyer represents in some other matter, even when the matters are wholly unrelated."

Still, any rather large-scale conflict of interest is unlikely to withstand scrutiny even if somehow formally waived away by a client and inexorably puts the attorney into a form of potential legal quicksand that can inevitably swallow them whole.

Now that we've established the conventional foundation for the lawyer-client conflict of interest proviso, let's punch things up a bit and contemplate the future of the law.

There is a strident belief that the use of Artificial Intelligence (AI) will gradually and ultimately change the nature of how the law is today being practiced.

At first, there will be AI that is considered semi-autonomous, meaning that it works hand-in-hand with human attorneys, providing an added capability as though a (nearly) fellow learned colleague was able to assist in legal undertakings. Further in the future, there will be fully autonomous AI that can serve not simply as an adjunct to a human attorney, but performs the same duties and legal capacities as a licensed human lawyer can.

Conflict Of Interest In AI Lawyer-Client Relationships

To be clear and also realistic, the days of an autonomous AI legal reasoning system that can perform equally as a human lawyer are a distant future. Do not rush out tomorrow and give up your law degree because of a false expectation that AI-enabled attorneys are going to take over your law practice any time soon.

Nonetheless, assuming that such a day will eventually arrive, we can consider the conflict of interest question as it relates to AI as the lawyering portion of the lawyer-client relationship.

Many are tempted to decry the idea of AI serving as such representation since it implies that opposing parties will be using the same AI system, creating a conflict of interest in the same manner as having the same human attorney representing opposing clients.

This is not quite as inevitable as might be portrayed by some.

One key aspect is to set aside the presumption that all AI is the same and a somehow monolith that is entirely interconnected. The odds are that the AI legal reasoning systems will differ from each other. Some will have a particular specialty of the law. Some will be provided by vendor X and another AI legal reasoning system will be from vendor Y, and so on.

Perhaps think of this as those chess playing online systems of today. You can readily have one chess-playing system be pitted against another one, something of wholly different mechanization. There is even a possibility of having one such chess system play against itself, though, in the case of an AI legal reasoning system, there would need to be put in place rigorous firewalls and other separations to ensure no leakage from one to the other.

Overall, the key point is that it is decidedly *not* axiomatic that we will have AI-based attorneys that are intrinsically intertwined and aflush with conflict of interest.

Conclusion

One final note.

Conflicts of interest are not necessarily always a blot upon society. As stated by Thomas Nixon Carver in his famous "Essays in Social Justice" of 1915: "The need for justice grows out of the conflict of human interests. That is to say, if there were no conflict of interests among mankind we should never have invented the word justice, nor conceived the idea for which it stands."

Seemingly, there are times when a conflict of interest is constructive, though, in the case of an adversarial form of adjudication and the role of legal representation, I think we can likely agree that excoriating any substantive conflict of interest is in the best interest of justice.

Even for a future of AI-based attorneys.

.

––––––––

Note: *For supplemental materials depicting the aspects discussed in this chapter, refer to Appendix B, which contains various augmented diagrams, charts, and additional related facets of relevance.*

CHAPTER 18

AI & LAW:
OVERZEALOUS LAWYERING

Key briefing points about this essay:

- Clients expect their attorney to be a vigorous and spirited legal representative

- This is also a requirement for the essence of our adversarial structure of justice

- But sometimes a lawyer goes overboard and stretches into being overzealous

- Overzealousness is a debatable threshold, nonetheless, sanctions can be applied

- In a future with AI-based attorneys, overzealousness (surprisingly) will still be at issue

Introduction

Most clients want a lawyer that will work vigorously and tirelessly for their cases (well, at least for the *particular* case of the said client). This is not simply a desirable trait, it is considered in fact a requirement to some degree as part of the duties of being an attorney.

Indeed, our adversarial approach to justice makes a core assumption that the legal representation for a client will strenuously and abundantly strive zealously in support of their client's legal posture. It is a fundamental premise that there will be a forceful representation, going head-to-head with equally forceful representation from the opposing side. If one side is less vigorous, potentially this undermines the position of the client so represented. That doesn't bode well for an adversarial structure.

Of course, there are limits to which this ardent vigor ought to go.

There is no doubt that some lawyers opt for a bridge too far in their spirited effort for a client. Often labeled as being overzealous, those lawyers veering beyond a somewhat vacuous line "that shall not be crossed" can be sanctioned for their over-the-top actions. What makes this a dicey proposition is that there is always the caveat that perhaps the attorney was doing their best for their client, exercising the type of forcefulness that is duty-bound, and the overabundance was ergo warranted.

As they say, art is in the eye of the beholder, and to some degree, the act of overzealousness is somewhat in the eye of the beholder too.

One form of an overzealous act is somewhat obvious, or at least less defensible when it contains curse words and profanity. This is the easiest of those instances that might be chastised as overzealous since they are immediately transparent and seemingly inexcusable. It is expected that a proper decorum will be maintained by attorneys in their role as an officer of the court. The use of foul language generally has no proper place in such discourse embodying expected civility.

Again, even this can be potentially given a free pass, assuming that the lingo was somewhat required or justified on a logical and professed rational basis. This is a bit of a slim tightrope, a fine line to hoe, and a difficult stance to achieve a green light given that the words are presumably damaging to sensibility and could be stated less outlandishly (though, the counterargument is that the shock value was purposeful and could not be depicted in any other equal way).

Another more subtle avenue of being overzealous consists of an attorney that proffers legal arguments that are without merit, considered seemingly frivolous on their face of what is being argued. If the position by an attorney is not consistent with the requirement that a legal argument ought to be legal or just, they may have fallen from the aims of our approach to justice. There is a primary assumption that attorneys will put forth good faith arguments, and thus simultaneously be averting bad faith arguments.

There are plentiful examples of human attorneys that were regarded as being overzealous and suffered various legal consequences accordingly. A recent case still underway provides a fascinating example of the range and nature of potential overzealous expression, namely in a lawsuit against the police that purportedly (by the attorneys representing the law enforcement agency) argue contains undue sarcasm, unnecessary slang, and was so verbose, confused, and redundant that its true substance, if any, was overly disguised (see "Sarcasm cut from police suit," by Elaine Goodman, *Daily Pilot*, January 4, 2021).

Let's shift gears and consider the future of the law, including how AI and the law will potentially play out over time.

Overzealousness For AI-Based Attorneys

There is an ongoing assumption that the use of Artificial Intelligence (AI) will gradually and ultimately change the nature of how the law is today being practiced. Initially, there will be AI that is considered semi-autonomous, meaning that it works hand-in-hand with human attorneys, providing an added capability as though a (nearly) fellow learned colleague was able to assist in legal undertakings. Further in the future, there will be fully autonomous AI that can serve not simply as an adjunct to a human attorney but perform the same duties and legal capacities as a licensed human lawyer can.

The days of an autonomous AI legal reasoning system that can perform equally as a human lawyer are a distant future. No need to start clearing out your desk at the office.

Upon achieving AI of that legal caliber, would it potentially verge on being overzealous?

Absolutely, this possibility would decidedly exist.

The assumption by many is that AI will be entirely dispassionate, acting in a well-mannered way and abiding strictly by the appropriate rules of legal propriety. Sorry to burst that bubble, but there is no such axiomatic basis to believe this will be the case.

Even today's variant of AI has been seen to emit curse words and other impolite utterances. Part of this is due to the use of Machine Learning and Deep Learning, computational pattern matching that lacks any semblance of common-sense reasoning. In a classic GIGO (garbage in, garbage out) mode, the computer simply reuses what it finds on the Internet and then spews out words that seem to be an integral part of our language and presumably a perfectly valid form of expression.

In that same vein, a future AI-based attorney might do likewise, and get caught in the overzealousness realm for rather noticeable and seemingly unacceptable language. Whether the AI can argue its way around being foul-mouthed will be on par with whether a human attorney can wiggle their way out of such a predicament.

On the aspect of potentially filing frivolous cases or otherwise making arguments that lack in good faith, this is also another possible foible for an AI-based legal reasoning system. Imagine a chess-playing computer that opts to come up with a series of chess moves that appear to be utterly devoid of proper protocol.

Consider these hefty questions:

- Has the AI found something beyond our own capacity to reason, or has it fallen into the trap of nonsensical argumentation?

- Does the posture of the AI-based attorney amount to frivolousness, or might there be a new avenue never before explored?

Conclusion

Just as a human attorney would likely fight bitterly against accusations of being overzealous, we ought to assume that an AI-based lawyer would do likewise.

Why so?

Because, as stated earlier, our adversarial approach to justice demands a forceful form of representation, and we would be doing ourselves a disservice if the AI variant was not up to that zealousness.

But, let's not have the AI go overboard, which it could, and we'll need to keep our eyes open and be ready to pushback, sanctioning the AI just we would sanction a human (well, kind of).

.

––––––––––

Note: *For supplemental materials depicting the aspects discussed in this chapter, refer to Appendix B, which contains various augmented diagrams, charts, and additional related facets of relevance.*

CHAPTER 19

AI & LAW:

HYRBRID NEURO-SYMBOLIC AI

Key briefing points about this essay:

- The use of Machine Learning (ML) continues to gain ground, including in the legal profession

- Many wonder whether the future of AI is entirely pegged to further advances solely in ML

- Some predict ML will hit a proverbial wall, and that rules-based approaches will be reborn

- These two camps (often warring) are known as the sub-symbolic and the symbolics

- A hybrid AI also referred to as neuro-symbolic, might be the way forward, for the law too

Introduction

It seems that the expanding use of AI is nearly unstoppable and will just keep going on a full-steam-ahead basis. This includes the use of AI in the law and for the legal profession, increasingly showing up as either integrated into modern LegalTech or provided as an amplifier or augmentation to conventional LegalTech.

What has spurred the wild ride toward AI can be laid at the feet of today's Machine Learning (ML) capabilities. ML is the hot buzzword and underlies much of the AI technology that you either hear about or are now making use of. It is assuredly the dawning of ML that is making the latest AI become a readily affordable and useable form of tech.

For proper clarification and acknowledgment, we can also include the continued miniaturization of computing, the emergence of cloud-based computer access, the decreasing costs of computing, the ever-spreading use of the Internet, and an overall grand convergence of numerous key high-tech factors that have helped propel AI into something that can be economically crafted and deployed.

Anyway, let's not distract from the allure of ML and let it stand tall.

There aren't any magical potions or otherworldly incantations involved in Machine Learning. A straightforward and relatively apt characterization is that ML is a form of computational pattern matching that mathematically tries to spot patterns in data and algorithmically reacts or is programmed to respond accordingly.

This ML-based pattern matching is oftentimes undertaken via the use of Artificial Neural Networks (ANN), a kind of biologically inspired variant of what we generally believe our wetware neurons do while inside the human brain, though please be aware that today's computer-based ANNs are demonstrably simpler and not at all like the real thing (as yet). Accepted parlance in the AI field is that these neural network simulations are considered a sub-symbolic kind of representation, suggesting that they are not particularly based on a higher-level symbolic or logic-based set of constructs and instead utilize a lower-level and quite granularly calculative approach.

Those of you that were around during an earlier heyday of AI might recall that there was a similar fervor about what AI could do or might be able to accomplish.

This was during the AI era that some refer to as the rules-based approach to AI, also known as the symbolic approach. Using so-called expert systems, also denoted as knowledge-based systems, the underlying precept was that it might be feasible to encapsulate human expertise or knowledge via the articulation of logic or rules and then codify said facets into a computer-based system.

Various limitations and seemingly insurmountable difficulties gradually made the initially touted rules-based path overly arduous and unlikely to achieve the ambitious aspirations first espoused. For example, trying to get human experts to somehow spill out their inner mental logic and unveil all of their assumed set of thinking rules was problematic in many ways. It took a lot of time to undertake, getting all of the rules surfaced was exceedingly tedious, and the resulting morass of presumed rules was unwieldy and considered brittle when it came to being used in real-world situations.

This led to a downtrodden period of AI that has earned the sour naming of the AI Winter, during which AI was placed onto the backburner and considered not especially viable or efficacious to pursue in daily use (albeit research continued in AI labs and on the academic front). The somewhat recent resurgence of AI, spurred by Machine Learning advances, has been labeled as the AI Spring, alluding to a seasonal Spring-like rebirth or rejuvenation for AI.

Given the aforementioned history as a revealing timeline of AI progress to-date, the most obvious and tantalizing question is what will happen next?

And, for our purposes herein, how will the presumed next generation or iteration of AI be relevant and additive to the use of AI in the law and for the legal profession?

The Next AI and the Legal Profession

Let's consult the AI crystal ball and see what it prophecies.

Some predict that the use of ML will become ubiquitous and reside in any tech that you might interact with, including those unseen systems, residing behind-the-scenes and for which you are involuntarily using. ML algorithms will get better and the training data needed to get them into suitable shape will be voluminously available and less costly to exploit.

That's the "more of the same" outlook for AI in the near future.

Others believe that ML is going to hit the proverbial wall. Just as expert systems and the rules-based camp ran into harsh and relatively unyielding blockages, so too will the ML and use of ANNs. The roadblocks won't necessarily be the same, yet nonetheless, there is a looming wall or barrier that will be the stopping point for further progress.

That is the "impenetrable sound barrier" outlook for AI.

There are also those of the (resentfully labeled) old-fashioned camp that assert we will see rebirth and emergence of the rules-based approach.

That is the "return of the Jedi" clamor.

I am an advocate of an incrementally growing vocal movement toward embracing the best of both worlds, namely combining judiciously the sub-symbolic and symbolic approaches. This is being referred to as neuro-symbolic or hybrid AI.

This is likely to be the decidedly prudent way to especially make further progress in the application of AI to the law. We can incorporate the rules-based aspects of the law and legal reasoning, along with the sub-symbolic ML and ANN avenues, which will enable breaking the barriers that each technique in of itself confronts. Such a one-two punch can overcome the qualms about sub-symbolic ML-based legal reasoning that is not duly transparent and lacking in interpretability and can meanwhile boost the symbolics side by providing the data-based surfacing ML benefits for discovering otherwise unsurfaced rules.

Conclusion

Perhaps the largest stumbling block will be overcoming the acute polarization between the seemingly (though needlessly so) opposite camps of the sub-symbolics versus the symbolics.

Maybe we need to construct an AI system to resolve that socially divisive conflict first.

––––––––––

Note: *For supplemental materials depicting the aspects discussed in this chapter, refer to Appendix B, which contains various augmented diagrams, charts, and additional related facets of relevance.*

CHAPTER 20

AI & LAW:

LAW SCHOOLS

Key briefing points about this essay:

- Few law schools offer a formal course on the topic of AI and the law

- Sometimes the AI and law topic haphazardly comes up during regular law classes

- There are bona fide reasons for adopting such classes and for opting to not do so

- The key arguments made on the pro and con side of this coin are equally compelling

- It would seem inevitable that someday this course will officially be at most law schools

Introduction

I'd be willing to bet that most lawyers did not take a formal class about the topic of AI and the law when they were churning their way through law school (there are some exceptions, but the rule-of-thumb is a relatively safe bet).

Perhaps somewhat surprisingly, even for those that just recently graduated or for those that are in the throes of law school right now the chances of formally learning about AI and the law is considered as remote a possibility as taking a trip to Mars.

Very few law schools offer a *formal* class that is focused *entirely* on the topic of AI and the law.

Some provide a directed studies class that might periodically switch from topic to topic, and perchance the focus of AI and law as an official possibility can haphazardly arise, though it is akin to being in Las Vegas at the slot machines as to when or if the class will materialize.

There are also law schools that offer a one-unit class that sits below the radar, probably something akin to an extended education offering, and let it generally rot on the vine, meaning that it exists to mainly have the appearance of providing such a class (this is not intended to denigrate those that mightily fight tooth-and-nail to get these mini-classes onto the schedule, doing so with the virtuous hopes that it might turn the tide toward greater recognition for a robust course offering).

Of course, there is also the sporadic covering of AI and the law that sometimes can arise during other more commonly expected and required law classes. Courses covering civil and criminal areas of the law might accidentally veer into the AI realm as a momentary offshoot, perhaps asking the students to read a particular paper or do some negligible research on the topic. That seems at least to be in the camp of "something is better than nothing" and could spark law students to pursue the topic on their own time. Unfortunately, this also inadvertently and inexorably allows for gross misunderstandings of what AI and the law is all about and proffers spotty grounding on this upcoming and altogether hefty topic.

I'll cover in a moment the reasons why such a class is not as yet on the formal docket of what is expected of law students.

Before explaining the basis both for and against having an official class on the AI and law topic, allow me to be aboveboard and express that I am an advocate for such a course to be offered. Just wanted to let you know that I have a dog in this hunt, as one might colloquially say, though you'll see in a moment my reasoning for taking such a posture.

That being said, I am assuredly not quite as fervent a proponent as some that adamantly argue it has to become a mandatory class for all law students everywhere. I think that seems a bridge too far, right now, though perhaps this might be sensible in the future. There is undoubtedly sound logic for some law schools to make this a mandatory class but doing so across the board for all law schools is a much tougher case to be made.

Covering Both Sides Of This Coin

With that preamble setting the stage, let's go ahead and cover the top reasons typically given for not offering an official class on AI and law (more reasons can certainly be divined):

- AI and the law as a full-blown topic is not yet ready for prime time. It is an interesting one and maybe, in about a decade or so, might be mature enough to warrant a closer look-see.

- It is a tech topic, but we are a law school. The coverage of AI and the law is out-of-place and would be better run in perhaps a computer science department rather than in a law school.

- We'd like to offer such a class and there are plenty of other trending topics to be added too, yet there is only so much time available and you cannot cram everything including the kitchen sink into the already jam-packed curriculum of key elements that law students need to know.

- Law students are ambitious and clever, so if they think the AI and law topic has merit, they will find a means to learn about it. No need to burden them with an outlier and ostensibly something that likely won't be covered when they take the bar exam.

- None of our faculty are familiar with AI and the law as a standalone topic. We try to let the faculty dovetail such material into their law classes if they wish to do so and if they, of their own volition, are willing to take upon themselves the extra effort to get up-to-speed.

Now the reasons in favor of a class on AI and the law:

- AI is the future of society, including that our laws will need to be adjusted and, in some ways, created anew to appropriately govern the advent of AI. Law students ought to be at the forefront of this and not caught unawares.

- The application of AI into the practice of law is already underway and will inexorably grow, thus, we need to prepare our law students so that they know when, why, and how to best use this emerging tech.

- Learning about AI and the law offers additional (surprising to some) benefits such as becoming more versed in legal argumentation and also the cognitive skills needed to demonstratively practice law.

- Producing law students in today's modern world that are seemingly illiterate when it comes to AI and the law is a disservice to those budding lawyers and undercuts the proper mission of a law school to prepare their flock for the future.

- AI is a hot topic and one that can be alluring to prospective law students, plus we don't want our existing law students to feel gipped that they missed the boat on a burgeoning area of the law.

That hopefully gives you a sense of the lay of the land on the pro and con of offering formal classes on AI and the law.

Conclusion

For those that insist that their law students "don't do computer programming" and that a law school has a higher mission than being a programmer mill, this sadly misstates and confuses what an appropriate AI and law class should be covering. Admittedly, sometimes a computer science professor is summarily roped into offering such a class, and of course they are likely going to teach what they know, such as software development, but that's not what a true AI and law class is all about.

We could carry on at length about the tradeoffs on this matter, so it might instead be best to set up an AI system to decide which way this ought to go, though only if that legally makes sense.

––––––––––

Note: *For supplemental materials depicting the aspects discussed in this chapter, refer to Appendix B, which contains various augmented diagrams, charts, and additional related facets of relevance.*

CHAPTER 21

AI & LAW:

CHICKEN OR THE EGG

Key briefing points about this essay:

- Which came first, the chicken or the egg?

- It seems that a compelling case can be made for either side, though argumentatively so

- An interesting likening to the advent of AI and the law raises akin infinite regress issues

- Ought the law be pointing fingers at the human that launched the AI or the AI itself

- A legal scholar has coined this the homunculus fallacy and warns to avoid sleight of hand

Introduction

You undoubtedly grew-up with at some point getting into a heated argument over the classic chicken-or-the-egg debate. Perhaps this happened while on the playground as a toddler. It might have resurfaced as a more interesting and intelligently debatable topic while in high school.

During your college days, it was the stuff of grand philosophical noodling and provided both delight and consternation in being resolvable.

Of course, some would assert that it is inarguably the egg that came first since you presumably cannot have a chicken without it being sprung from an egg. Case closed. Well, the other side exhorts, a chicken was seemingly required to produce that egg, and therefore the chicken had to come first, else there would not be an egg in existence.

Yikes, this is rather perplexing and a bit of a paradox.

This is not a new paradox and can be dated to at least the days of Aristotle. One response to the vexing question is to state that an all-knowing omnipresent entity made chickens and thereafter this generated the egg-to-chicken infinite series.

Most scientists would point out that the first eggs seem to have appeared on planet Earth long before chickens came around. Furthermore, the chicken is said to be a variant or somewhat of a descendent of birds, and thusly you could claim that a bird laid an egg that became a chicken. That seems to solve it, the egg came first, and the chicken came thereafter.

This analytical answer though does not quite seem to resolve the matter since you can certainly ask, perhaps somewhat indignantly, what created a bird. Where and how did the first bird arise? And so on we can go.

You might be familiar with a famous rule known as the infinite regress and for which the chicken-and-the-egg provides a handy foil for discussing the lofty topic of things that are infinite in series.

The notion of infinite regress is typically taught in courses about logic and oftentimes also covered in mathematical theories classes. You can start with some declared proposition and say that if it is true then a next in line proposition is also true. In turn, there is the next proposition after that next one, and so on, ad infinitum.

This series of steps are logically predicated on each other and can continue forever, potentially if so applicable. That viewpoint involves pondering the series from its alleged start to the potential end (or, never-ending end, as it were), and we are usually willing to accept the notion that it might continue on an infinite basis.

If you jump into the series at some midway point, you might be stumped as to what started the darn thing, to begin with. You assume that there must be a start that spawned all the rest of the series. The twist is that you might not ever be able to trace the series to whatever started it and can only shrug your shoulders and accept that the series exists. Some would even philosophically argue that there does not necessarily need to have been a start at all (no spurring cause) and that perhaps the matter stretches back infinitely, ergo it is futile and mistaken to search for a singular form of a so-called beginning.

Shifting gears, let's see how this conundrum applies to the law, and particularly the role underlying AI and the law.

The Human-Or-The-AI Conundrum

When a human commits a faulty act, we normally hold that person responsible for their actions. Sure, there are lots of potential exceptions, but go with me that generally, this is a reasonable truism.

Someone decides to craft an AI system. The person puts this AI system into use. Suppose the AI system commits a faulty act.

Who or what is responsible?

The accusatory finger seems to assuredly point at the person that crafted the AI. We would naturally assume that whoever crafted something ought to be held responsible for the actions of the thing that they made. Hitting someone with a stick seems to suggest that the person wielding the stick is the culprit, rather than the stick itself (a stick presumably has no mind of its own).

There is an ongoing debate about whether AI is a stick or more like a human.

This is the crux of the legal personhood question that sits at the heart of recent debates about our laws and whether existing laws can cope with AI that might be autonomous (as an important side note, there isn't any AI yet that is sentient).

Some legal scholars argue that anyone looking at the AI is being tricked, similar to a magic act where the elephant disappears seemingly on its own and you weren't watching the magician and their sleight of hand. Professor Jack Balkin of the Yale Law School mentions in his provocative article entitled "The Three Laws of Robotics in the Age of Big Data" (*Ohio State Law Journal*, 2017): "Instead of focusing on laws directed at robots (or algorithms), I focus on laws directed at the people who program and use robots, AI agents, and algorithms. That is because what we need in the emerging Algorithm Society are not laws of robotics, but laws of robot operators."

He has labeled the distraction of looking at the AI as the *homunculus fallacy*: "The homunculus fallacy is the belief that there is a little person inside the program who is making it work—it has good intentions or bad intentions, and it makes the program do good or bad things. But in fact, there is no little person inside the algorithm. There is programming—code—and there is data. And the program uses the data to run, with good or bad effects, some predictable, some unpredictable. When we criticize algorithms, we are really criticizing the programming, or the data, or their interaction. But equally important, we are also criticizing the use to which they are being put by the humans who programmed the algorithms, collected the data, or employed the algorithms and the data to perform particular tasks."

The counterargument has to do with that troublesome chicken-or-egg question.

If a human produces AI, and suppose the AI varies itself by "learning" as it goes, should the human that started things be still held responsible?

Imagine too that a human crafts AI, which let's assume begets additional AI, and we continue this for a lengthy series. At some iteration long beyond the start, do we still go back to the beginning to find the responsible party, or do we decide it is somewhere in the series, and therefore ultimately it is the AI that gets pinned with the tail on the donkey?

Conclusion

They say that infinite regress can be either virtuous or vicious, and thus while stewing over the mindbending chicken-or-the-egg, maybe include likewise human-or-the-AI into your deep thinking of where responsibility resides.

Note: *For supplemental materials depicting the aspects discussed in this chapter, refer to Appendix B, which contains various augmented diagrams, charts, and additional related facets of relevance.*

CHAPTER 22

AI & LAW:

LEGAL JARGON

Key briefing points about this article:

- Legalese or legal jargon is oftentimes criticized by both non-lawyers and lawyers alike

- There is a case to be made for the basis of having legal language and specialized lingo

- Nonetheless, there is concern about the use of so-called lawyering "weasel words"

- Some seem to believe or hope that the adoption of AI in the law will obviate such lingo

- It is argued herein that this is a false assumption and quite unlikely an outcome of AI use

Introduction

Trying to make sense of a legal contract can be disheartening and exceedingly exasperating for those that are not versed in the language of the law. Surprisingly, perhaps, even those trained and experienced in the lingo of the law, such as lawyers, judges, and the like, are at times frustrated by the use of legal jargon or assert that it is overused and exploited.

To the everyday ear, words such as "thereof" and "whereby" seem exceedingly haughty and appear to be employed simply to showcase piety over normal folks. What really gets the goat of many people is the lawyering lingo that has all the earmarks of being purposefully vague and, well, altogether weaselly, as in the use of weasel words.

The complaint about weasel words is that they tend to provide wiggle room and do not definitively layout what they portend to mean. For example, the classic phrase of "including but not limited to" is seen as one of those pufferies that exists to provide some undisclosed escape hatch and yet bandied about to insidiously appear as crisp and solid, when in actual fact it is a colossal loophole laying in waiting.

Of course, such words and phrases can be readily defended as necessary and just.

If someone said that something ostensibly was "including X, Y, and Z" and then at a later point in time there was a relevant R that arose, the immediate argument to be made is that the allegedly missing R was never in the original list of things mentioned (only the X, Y, and Z were delineated) and therefore the R does not belong therein. By instead proffering that the list was "including but not limited to X, Y, and Z" there is an abundantly sensible and reasonable indication that someday there might be something else pertinent, which later on perchance it happens to be a previously unknown or merely unstated R, and the case can be made that R is now nonetheless rightfully a member of that "not limited to" original list.

The usual counterargument would be that if you wanted R to be included, by gosh, you should have listed it to start with, as in "including X, Y, Z, and R" as the proper showcase of what you meant to say. The counter to the counterargument is that it might not have been known that R was ultimately encapsulated and therefore unfair to have insisted that the list itself must be entirely complete and exhaustive at the get-go.

Round and round this merry-go-round can proceed.

For those of you interested in the words used in the law, I can highly recommend one of my favorite books on the topic, namely "The Language of the Law" by David Mellinkoff, which was published in 2004 and provides a fascinating look at the history and roots of modern-day legal wording. If you wondered how various Latin words and phrases have remained intact over the storied history of the law, he provides interesting examples of how they have been at times retained as originally intended while in other instances twisted and bent beyond the shape of the meaning they once had.

In any case, rather than stoking flames by claiming these are weasel words, some prefer to emphasize that these are the proper and prudent ways of lawyerly speaking and therefore are suitably referred to as legal parlance, or legal language, the language of jurisprudence, legal lingo, legalistic jargon and simply the argot or vernacular of the law.

Case closed, as they say.

Shifting gears, let's consider the future of the law.

There are signs that ultimately the use of Artificial Intelligence (AI) will gradually and inevitably be woven into the nature of the law and the daily practice of the law.

This is beginning to happen now, though these are only the early days of AI-based infusion and there is still a long way to go before we'll be witnessing autonomous AI-based legal reasoning as part of our judicial ways and mores.

AI and the Language of the Law

Some have proclaimed that a handy benefit of using AI in the law is that we'll finally dispense with all of those weasel words that have permeated the law. I am not sure why this is believed, and it is undeniably a head-scratching assumption, for sure.

Perhaps the reasoning is that the AI systems that can fully undertake legal reasoning will find themselves disgusted at the so-called weasel words and decide that it is time to do a sorely needed clean-up. If so, that's a bit of anthropomorphizing of AI that is over-the-top and a dreamy notion for those that have a rabid distaste for legalese.

Another possibility for this outsized belief is that AI is viewed by some as though it is always strictly precise and conclusive in what it spouts and does. As such, either AI will straighten out these weasel words, or perhaps we will all be forced to reconstitute legal jargon if we want to have AI participate in any truly autonomous manner.

Sorry to burst the bubble on this matter, but the advent of AI in the law will have a negligible impact on the prevalence of legal vernacular.

Here's why:

- Legal jargon serves a purpose, providing useful legal devices, and has already been tested and reinforced throughout its course of semantic twists and turns. AI will not somehow magically overturn that intrinsic human language.

- The language of the law is an accepted practice and provides a customary and expected means of describing and depicting the law. AI in the law will be devised as a proper mainstay of the law and legal practice, therefore it will surely be established to use the prevailing legalese (a form of dismal corruption, some might bemoan).

- There are no clear cut and absolutely unambiguous replacements that would miraculously eviscerate the need for flexibility in expressing legal matters. Humans themselves struggle with finding suitable replacements for the "weasel words" and thus there is little basis to assume that AI will mystically do any better at doing so (even if there is a superhuman version of AI, which nobody knows what or if such automata will materialize).

Conclusion

There is also a notion that perhaps AI will eventually no longer need humans in the law, overtaking the need for human lawyers and human judges, and can ergo opt to create whatever new lingo it wishes to use (a precise, mathematical formulation, evidently). I have serious doubts about this prophesied outcome.

Then again, perhaps someday in the future we will be pointing accusatory fingers at AI and exhorting that it is using way too many darned weasel words.

———————

Note: *For supplemental materials depicting the aspects discussed in this chapter, refer to Appendix B, which contains various augmented diagrams, charts, and additional related facets of relevance.*

CHAPTER 23

AI & LAW:
LEGAL CHESS PLAYING

Key briefing points about this essay:

- Some liken the practice of law to the playing of chess

- Lawyers need to conceive of their legal moves and countermoves related to opposing counsel

- AI chess-playing systems have gotten quite good and there are lessons to be learned therein

- It is handy to consider the state-space complexity in the construct of legal argumentation

- Predictions are that the use of AI legal reasoning will ultimately be integral to legal arguments

Introduction

The odds are pretty high that you know the name Bobby Fischer, considered one of the greatest chess players ever.

Anyone with small children that play chess is apt to have told their offspring that someday they might be as good at chess as Bobby was. It seems that every time a youngster even appears to play chess well, adults begin to refer to the child as yet another Bobby Fischer.

In the entertaining and informative movie *Searching for Bobby Fischer*, there is a refrain repeated several times, consisting of the stern admonishment to the chess-playing child prodigy in the story: "Don't move until you see it." This might seem like an obvious piece of advice, namely, to think before you act, but the rub is that these chess matches are a nail-biting timeboxed event and for each moment of not taking your turn the clock is winding down. Seconds and ostensibly split seconds can end-up being the difference between winning and losing a timed chess match. In that sense, if you are thinking during your turn, when you are on the clock, as it were, you'd better think fast.

The problem with thinking fast is that it can inextricably equate with not thinking completely or otherwise shortcutting the thinking process.

Therein lays the conundrum. If you are willing to undercut your thinking time, you'll save those precious seconds, perhaps needing them later on. But this also leads to the possibility that you are making a somewhat rash move that was not especially thoughtful, perhaps a dreadful move that will ultimately put you into a losing checkmate, and ergo having saved time was counterproductive in the end.

One advantage for lawyers and the act of lawyering is that you are seldom on the clock, at least not in the same manner as a traditional chess match (as an aside, chess is classified as a two-player zero-sum "perfect information" game that has no hidden info about the gameplay per se, i.e., all actual moves are seen by both players).

Sure, when standing before the judge and arguing your case, there is a devout semblance of time being of the essence. If you are asked a question and cannot reply with a rapid and sensible response, it makes you seem ill-prepared and also implies that your loss for words arises because your case is decidedly weak and there isn't any suitably defensible reply to be had.

Those moments of tension and time-based stress are as real as those when sitting at a chessboard and having to ascertain what move is best to make.

Shifting gears, let's consider what happens during chess playing and leverage what we know from the application of AI to chess-playing to see if the same fundamentals can be applied to the act of lawyering.

Indeed, there are predictions that we will ultimately have AI applied to the law and the practice of law that is capable of directly assisting human lawyers, including eventually reaching truly autonomous AI legal reasoning. In the case of autonomous legal reasoning, it is presumed that this kind of AI could potentially take on the role of a lawyer, a judge, and other legal professionals, operating without the need for any human assistance.

AI, Chess, and the Practice of Law

With that preamble, let's unpack the AI chess playing insights.

When playing a game like chess, each move is referred to as a ply. I make a move, and then you make a countermove, which means we are now two-ply into the match. When I made my original move, hopefully, I was anticipating the possible countermoves that you would make. I don't know for sure what move you will opt to do, though I can possibly make mental guesses.

For example, I can guess that you won't make a move that seems entirely like an outright blunder. Unless you've never played chess before, you are likely to realize that you need to protect your king, and thus if you immediately make a move that puts your king at risk, this will seem foolhardy and I would not anticipate your doing so. Of course, it could be a trick, lulling me into believing that you are doing something amiss, and possibly seeking to catch me off-guard accordingly.

If you have not yet thought about the number of moves and countermoves that can occur in a game of chess, it is a really large number.

This is worth mentioning because some people wonder why you don't just imagine in your mind all of the possible moves, and then you would be ready for any move that your opponent makes. In theory, you could play, in your mind, all possible games of chess, and when you are in the midst of chess competition, you can already have a map that shows what might happen next, along with ascertaining which move you should make to in the long run reach a win.

The state-space complexity or number of possibilities is enormous. A famous mathematician named Claude Shannon in 1950 proposed that it is something like 10 to the 120th power in size (referred to today as the Shannon number). The estimated number of stars in the known and observable universe is around 10 to the 23rd power, thus many magnitudes less than the number of chess move combinations. The number of atoms in the universe is estimated at 10 the 82nd power, which is, astoundingly, many magnitudes less than the chess state-space.

The good news for lawyers is that you seldom are going to have a legal case that has the same enormity of potential moves or state-space (though it might seem like it!).

Nonetheless, just as in chess, it is important to consider your move, the likely countermoves, and your best choice for countering the countermoves, and so on.

This is why the use of AI in the law is being seen as a potential boon for preparing legal arguments. A human lawyer might not be willing or able to envision the multitude of potential moves and countermoves, while an AI-based legal reasoning system could potentially do so with ease. This could aid lawyers in thinking through their case, along with averting the potential oopsie or having failed to consider a legal argument that their opponent suddenly brandishes and catches one legally by surprise.

Conclusion

The next time you are before the bench and find yourself at a loss for words because you had not considered a suddenly introduced legal argument, you might find yourself relishing the day that your handy dandy AI-based legal reasoning system will be at your side and able to proffer the best chess-like move to win the legal case at hand.

.

Note: *For supplemental materials depicting the aspects discussed in this chapter, refer to Appendix B, which contains various augmented diagrams, charts, and additional related facets of relevance.*

CHAPTER 24

AI & LAW:

SETTING THE BAR ON PROFICIENCY

Key briefing points about this essay:

- Consider the difficulties of trying to rate and compare new movies

- This can be done by contrasting with ones that same year, or all-time, or versus perfection

- Shifting gears, AI-based legal reasoning systems will gradually be introduced and utilized

- The proficiency of such AI systems to practice law will certainly come into question

- This raises the matter of rating, AI versus AI, or AI versus human lawyering, or perfection

Introduction

A fun or certainly provocative way to start a conversation involves mentioning a recently released film and then making some bold statement about whether it was a wonderous film or launch into trashing the movie and claim it was a worthless use of film.

The odds are that you'll get a reaction out of whomever you discuss the flick with (be careful, this could spark fisticuffs).

If the film was a sequel, the odds are that you compared the latest incarnation with the original movie. Seems like sequels oftentimes do not live up to the expectations created by a really strong first film. You might decide that a better comparison involves rating the movie against other recent ones that have come out in the last year or so.

For those movie watchers that are film buffs, they would likely make a comparison to older movies and try to showcase their encyclopedic knowledge about prior flicks. This could also lead you down the path of contrasting this new movie with a ranking of the top ten of all-time films.

Amidst all these comparisons, would you try to also assess the new movie on a basis of whether it was a *perfect* film?

That seems a bit challenging to do.

What exactly is a so-called perfect film?

One claim would be that a perfect movie was one that had a lot of people watch it, but this assertion is rather flimsy because there are movies rated as "best ever" by well-known film critics that did not vault into the most-watched listings per se. In that case, maybe you would be willing to accept whatever the film critics insist is a perfect movie, though that's problematic since you aren't going to get universal agreement on such an amorphous notion.

Perfection, in this case, can be ostensibly said to be in the eye of the beholder.

Keep that in mind as it will be a crucial point in a moment herein.

Shifting gears, let's discuss the advent of Artificial Intelligence (AI) in the law. There is going to be an increasing adoption of AI toward undertaking aspects of legal reasoning. We are still in the infancy of such use, but you can pretty much bet your bottom dollar that this trend is going to continue and indeed quicken in its pace and scope.

Figuring Out AI Legal Proficiency

At some point, AI as applied to the practice of law will eventually reach a level of proficiency that is demonstrative. Lawyers will rely upon an AI-based legal reasoning system to aid them in crafting their legal arguments. Judges might have at their fingertips an AI-powered judicial system that assists in the adjudication process and participates actively in composing rulings. Some assert that the AI will progress to a capability of working autonomously, thus, in a sense, the AI will be standalone as a lawyer and able to function without a human mind or hand at the ready.

If you came upon such an AI-based legal reasoning system and wanted to tell a friend or colleague about the aptitude of the system, what would you say?

Recall that when extolling the virtues or the imperfections of a newly released movie, you compared the movie to others already in existence. Okay, so maybe one means to rate or rank an AI-based legal reasoning system would be how it compares to other akin AI systems that are already available at that time. This is interesting and seemingly useful, though it doesn't especially help since the prior ones might be quite wimpy and this new one is only slightly less wimpy.

It seems that we ought to have a lower boundary and an upper boundary that could be used to assess our belief in the capability of an AI system that is being used in the law.

The easiest construct would certainly seem to be the upper boundary condition, namely that we could stipulate that an AI legal reasoning system ought to reach legal perfection and that's when we'd be really satisfied with it. Unfortunately, this brings up an earlier open-ended matter. How do you define perfection in this context?

In essence, assume that we are rating human lawyers and you wanted to establish a topmost position on a scale that had the so-called *perfect lawyer* as its pinnacle. If we can agreeably come up with that definition, all we need to do is then assert that an AI-based lawyer needs to achieve that same vaunted aspiration.

Well, I'll leave it to you as a mental exercise to conjure up an ironclad definition of "perfection" for what a *perfect lawyer* constitutes (and don't just start naming yourself or your revered partners).

Good luck with that.

Perhaps we can noodle on that notion and meanwhile take a look at the lower boundary instead. What is the minimum proficiency for someone or something that is seeking to claim the label or title of being a lawfully authorized lawyer?

We can use the ABA criteria which indicates that generally there is a need to pass a state bar exam, possess a bachelor's degree or equivalent, complete an accredited law school program, pass a character test and a fitness review, take an oath, and receive a license from the highest court in that state.

Should that be the lower boundary for an autonomous AI-based legal reasoning system that would potentially be used as a lawyer by the public and for which no human lawyer is needed to aid in the system and its usage?

Setting aside the academic credentials for the AI, would you feel comfortable saying that an AI system that could pass the bar has met the minimum requirements needed to practice law?

That is a readily debatable notion.

Conclusion

Just as there are often verbal fights over which movie is good or lousy, you can certainly expect that pronounced skirmishes are going to arise about letting AI systems act as attorneys (the stakes are enormously high). Determining the lower boundary is going to be agonizing, and likewise, even the topmost post is going to be immensely arguable.

For those that are hopeful of stopping AI from getting the legal imprimatur to practice law, maybe holdout that only once AI reaches legal perfection and has achieved *perfect lawyer* status can it be admitted to the bar, which might set the bar so high that it will be eons before AI gets the nod, if eve.

Note: *For supplemental materials depicting the aspects discussed in this chapter, refer to Appendix B, which contains various augmented diagrams, charts, and additional related facets of relevance.*

CHAPTER 25

AI & LAW:
REPEATEDLY TRYING IS SANE

Key briefing points about this essay:

- Popular these days is that repeatedly doing something is insane if expecting a differing result

- Claimed as attributable to Einstein, there is no indication he said this

- Furthermore, as an alleged truism, it is misleading and faulty

- This comes up since it is being used by skeptics that doubt the efficacy of AI in the law

- They fail to realize that there are under-the-hood differences, thus premature exhortations

Introduction

You might know someone that has a either T-shirt or a mug emblazoned with a popular saying that seems to be making the rounds and gaining its own fifteen minutes of fame. The saying is that the definition of insanity is doing the same thing over and over again and yet expecting different results.

Furthermore, to try and boost the authoritative air of this catchy assertion, those uttering the juicy point will in a snooty manner add that this witticism was a favored line by Albert Einstein. This provides a shield of invincibility to the now-infamous remark since only a fool would somehow doubt or question the wisdom of Einstein.

Time to unpack and eviscerate this popular and altogether misleading quip.

First, there is no bona fide evidence that Einstein ever spoke those words.

Researchers have dug deep to try and find someplace at some time that he might have mentioned this catchphrase or even said something remotely similar, and the result so far is a big zilch. You might insist that just because it can't be found as something he did say, you can't disprove that he never said it. Well, yes, there is no viable means to prove that he never said it, since we would have to find and scour a tape recording of every word that he voiced during his entire lifetime. I ask you this, doesn't it stand to reason that if he did say the utterance there would be some kind of documented evidence?

In short, you can continue to contend that it was said by Einstein, if that's what you want to do, though keep in mind that you are on quite shaky ground, and when push comes to shove there is no reliable indication that he actually said it. On a reasonableness basis, it seems prudent to refrain from claiming that it is an Einstein quote (you could try to be hazy and give yourself some slippage, rolling your eyes a bit and offering that some say that he said it).

Okay, so remove the Einstein invincibility cloak.

You might argue that it doesn't matter who said it since it otherwise is a devout truism and stands resolutely and independently on its own two legs.

Let's poke some holes into the alleged truism properties.

Having worked with one of the founders of Pandora, I know by heart his popular telling that when first trying to pitch the startup to potential investors, he and his co-founders tried repeatedly to get investor interest but failed time and again to get any dough. How many times would you be willing to pitch a startup idea that was at the time completely new and for which no one thought made any sense? Maybe twenty times? Perhaps even fifty times? Certainly, after one hundred pitches you would see the light, realize that everyone is exhorting that it is a rotten idea, and you'd give up or ostensibly abandon the idea and switch to some alternative.

After about the two hundredth pitch, an investor finally said yes. The funding was provided, and of course today we know how amazing a tremendous success Pandora became, plus it launched an entirely new segment of the marketplace.

Why have I told you this uplifting story?

Because, turning back the clock, you could have told the Pandora founders at say pitch number seventy-five that the definition of insanity is doing the same thing repeatedly and expecting a different result. Presumably, they were "insane" for believing that they had something innovative and worthwhile. Were they? History indubitably shows they were right in their belief.

The point is that you might rightfully be doing the same thing, over and over, and regrettably keep getting one undesirable result, such as the mile-high pile of no's that the Pandora entrepreneurs got during the two hundred pitches, meanwhile expecting or hoping for that *one different result*, a blissful yes that finally arose. This doesn't seem like insanity, by any means. It can be doggedness, it can be considered determination, and you could say that at times it is perhaps foolhardy but tossing the entire kit and kaboodle into the insanity bucket is seemingly equally foolhardy.

This is not to imply that if you are getting the same result and wish to get a different result then it isn't worthwhile to reconsider what you are doing. This seems like a rational form of thinking. You need to assess the tradeoff of changing versus not changing, and whether the desired result is going to be any closer or further from your aspirational reach accordingly.

In a nutshell, an outright condemnation of axiomatically being wrong when doing something repeatedly and expecting a different result is wholly misleading and can be decidedly poor advice though presumably being given with sincerity.

AI In The Law Are Bona Fide Attempts

Shifting gears, consider another recent example of using this same line by those that are seemingly undercutting researchers and developers that are adamantly toiling away at infusing Artificial Intelligence (AI) into the law.

As helpful background, there are a multitude of efforts underway to imbue legal reasoning into AI systems. The initial focus involves AI that can assist lawyers, while longer-term the aim is to have AI that autonomously performs lawyering tasks without any human involvement.

Anyway, skeptics nowadays are saying that these efforts to infuse AI into the law and the practice of law are repeating futile attempts. You can trace such legal infusing struggles to the initial days of the advent of AI systems, dating back to the 1950s and 1960s. Given that we don't yet have an AI-based lawyer walking around, the claim is that this is a research pursuit that showcases the notion of doing the same thing repeatedly and yet expecting different results.

This highlights another falsehood about the revered line. Sometimes there is an assumption that the same thing is being repeatedly undertaken, when in fact under-the-hood a differing approach is being used. Advances in AI capabilities of Natural Language Processing and Machine Learning are among the many changes that suggest a different result might well be achievable, namely the emergency of first semi-autonomous AI lawyering and then later on autonomous.

Conclusion

One last gripe about the deceptive line. Bandying around the word "insanity" is a disservice to the meaning of the word (legally and in a broader sense too), and though it is obviously being used in a somewhat joking manner, it would be nice to switch to some other wording.

Perhaps the entire phrase can be disregarded, or maybe eventually will wear out its welcome and we'll no longer be inundated with it, which means there are a bunch of mugs in the office that will need to be tossed out sooner or later. I'll start now.

.

———

Note: *For supplemental materials depicting the aspects discussed in this chapter, refer to Appendix B, which contains various augmented diagrams, charts, and additional related facets of relevance.*

APPENDIX A
TEACHING WITH THIS MATERIAL
AND BIBLIOGRAPHY

The essays in this book can readily be used as a reading supplemental to augment traditional textbook-oriented content, particularly used in a class on AI or a class about the law.

Courses where this material is most likely applicable encompass classes at a college or university level.

Here are some typical settings that might apply:

o <u>Computer Science</u>. Classes studying AI, or possibly a CS social impacts class, etc.

o <u>Law</u>. Law classes exploring technology and its adoption for legal uses.

o <u>Sociology</u>. Sociology classes on the adoption and advancement of technology.

Specialized classes at the undergraduate and graduate level can also make use of this material.

For each chapter, consider whether you think the chapter provides material relevant to your course topic.

There are plenty of opportunities to get the students thinking about the topics and encourage them to decide whether they agree or disagree with the points offered and positions taken.

I would also encourage you to have the students do additional research beyond the chapter material presented (I provide next some suggested assignments that they can do).

RESEARCH ASSIGNMENTS ON THESE TOPICS

Your students can find research and background material on these topics, doing so in various tech journals, law journals, and other related publications.

Here are some suggestions for homework or projects that you could assign to students:

a) <u>Assignment for foundational AI research topics</u>: Research and prepare a paper and a presentation on a specific aspect of AI, such as Machine Learning, ANN, etc. The paper should cite at least 3 reputable sources. Compare and contrast to what has been stated in the chosen chapter.

b) <u>Assignment for Law topics</u>: Research and prepare a paper covering Law aspects via at least 3 reputable sources and analyze the characterizations. Compare and contrast to what has been stated in the chosen chapter.

c) <u>Assignment for a Business topic</u>: Research and prepare a paper and a presentation on businesses and advanced technology regarding AI and Law. What is trending, and why? Make sure to cite at least 3 reputable sources. Compare and contrast to the depictions herein.

d) <u>Assignment to do a Startup:</u> Have the students prepare a paper or business plan about how they might start up a business in this realm. They could also be asked to present their business plan and should also have a prepared presentation deck to coincide with it.

You can certainly adjust the aforementioned assignments to fit your particular needs and class structure.

You'll notice that I usually suggest that (at least) 3 reputable cited sources be utilized for the paper writing-based assignments.

I usually steer students toward "reputable" publications, since otherwise, they will cite some less reliable sources that have little or no credentials, other than that they happened to appear online was easy to retrieve. You can, of course, define "reputable" in whatever way you prefer, for example, some faculty think Wikipedia is not reputable while others believe it is reputable and allow students to cite it.

The reason that I usually ask for at least 3 citations is that if the student only relies upon one or two citations, they usually settle on whatever they happened to find the fastest. By requiring 3 (or more) citations, it usually seems to inspire them to explore more extensively and likely end-up finding five or more sources, and then whittling it down to 3 if so needed.

I have not specified the length of their papers and leave that to you to tell the students what you prefer.

For each of those assignments, you could end up with a short one to two-pager or you could do a dissertation length in-depth paper. Base the length on whatever best fits for your class, and likewise the credit amount of the assignment within the context of the other grading metrics you'll be using for the class.

I usually try to get students to present their work, in addition to doing the writing. This is a helpful practice for what they will do in the business world. Most of the time, they will be required to prepare an analysis and present it. If you don't have the class time or inclination to have the students present their papers, then you can presumably omit the aspect of them putting together presentations.

GUIDE TO USING THE CHAPTERS

For each of the chapters, I provide the next some various ways to use the chapter contents.

You can assign the below tasks as individual homework assignments, or the tasks can be used for team projects. You can easily layout a series of assignments, such as indicating that the students are to do item "a" below for say Chapter 1, then "b" for the next chapter of the book, and so on.

a) What is the main point of the chapter and describe in your own words the significance of the topic.

b) Identify at least two aspects in the chapter that you agree with and support your concurrence by providing at least one other outside researched item as support; make sure to explain your basis for agreeing with the aspects.

c) Identify at least two aspects in the chapter that you disagree with and support your disagreement by providing at least one other outside researched item as support; make sure to explain your basis for disagreeing with the aspects.

d) Find an aspect that was not covered extensively in the chapter, doing so by conducting outside research, and then offer an expanded indication about how that aspect ties into the chapter, along with the added significance it brings to the topic.

e) Interview a specialist in the industry about the topic of the chapter, collect from them their thoughts and opinions, and readdress the chapter by citing your source and how they compared and contrasted to the material,

f) Interview a relevant professor or researcher in a college or university setting about the topic of the chapter, collect from them their thoughts and opinions, and readdress the chapter by citing your source and how they compared and contrasted to the material,

g) Try to update a chapter by finding out the latest on the topic and ascertain whether the issue or topic has now been solved or whether it is still being addressed, explain what you come up with.

The above are all ways in which you can get the students of your class involved in considering the material of a given chapter. You could mix things up by having one of those above assignments per each week, covering the chapters over the course of the semester or quarter.

SUGGESTED REFERENCES TO EXPLORE

To help get your students started in finding relevant and important papers on the topic of AI and the law, I provide next a handy bibliography that can be utilized.

You could also assign the students to each (or in teams) read an assigned reference from the list, and then have them provide either a written summary and review or do so as part of a classroom presentation.

BIBLIOGRAPHIC REFERENCES

1. Aleven, Vincent (1997). "Teaching Case-Based Argumentation Through a Model and Examples," Ph.D. Dissertation, University of Pittsburgh.

2. Aleven, Vincent (2003). "Using Background Knowledge in Case-Based Legal Reasoning: A Computational Model and an Intelligent Learning Environment," Artificial Intelligence.

3. Amgoud, Leila (2012). "Five Weaknesses of ASPIC+," Volume 299, Communications in Computer and Information Science (CCIS).

4. Antonious, Grigoris, and George Baryannis, Sotiris Batsakis, Guido Governatori, Livio Robaldo, Givoanni Siragusa, Ilias Tachmazidis (2018). "Legal Reasoning and Big Data: Opportunities and Challenges," August 2018, MIREL Workshop on Mining and Reasoning Legal Texts.

5. Ashley, Kevin (1991). "Reasoning with Cases and Hypotheticals in HYPO," Volume 34, International Journal of Man-Machine Studies.

6. Ashley, Kevin, and Karl Branting, Howard Margolis, and Cass Sunstein (2001). "Legal Reasoning and Artificial Intelligence: How Computers 'Think' Like Lawyers," Symposium: Legal Reasoning and Artificial Intelligence, University of Chicago Law School Roundtable.

7. Baker, Jamie (2018). "A Legal Research Odyssey: Artificial Intelligence as Disrupter," Law Library Journal.

8. Batsakis, Sotiris, and George Baryannis, Guido Governatori, Illias Tachmazidis, Grigoris Antoniou (2018). "Legal Representation and Reasoning in Practice: A Critical Comparison," Volume 313, Legal Knowledge and Information Systems.

9. Bench-Capon, Trevor (2004). "AGATHA: Automation of the Construction of Theories in Case Law Domains," January 2004, Legal Knowledge and Information Systems Jurix 2004, Amsterdam.

10. Bench-Capon, Trevor (2012). "Representing Popov v Hayashi with Dimensions and Factors," March 2012, Artificial Intelligence and Law.

11. Bench-Capon, Trevor, and Givoanni Sartor (2003). "A Model of Legal Reasoning with Cases Incorporating Theories and Values," November 2013, Artificial Intelligence.

12. Breuker, Joost (1996). "A Functional Ontology of Law," October 1996, ResearchGate.

13. Bruninghaus, Stefanie, and Kevin Ashley (2003). "Combining Case-Based and Model-Based Reasoning for Predicting the Outcome of Legal Cases," June 2003, ICCBR'03: Proceedings of the 5th International Conference on Case-based reasoning: Research and Development.

14. Buchanan, Bruce, and Thomas Headrick (1970). "Some Speculation about Artificial Intelligence and Legal Reasoning," Volume 23, Stanford Law Review.

15. Chagal-Feferkorn, Karni (2019). "Am I An Algorithm or a Product: When Products Liability Should Apply to Algorithmic Decision-Makers," Stanford Law & Policy Review.

16. Douglas, William (1948). "The Dissent: A Safeguard of Democracy," Volume 32, Journal of the American Judicature Society.

17. Dung, P, and R. Kowalski, F. Toni (2006). "Dialectic Proof Procedures for Assumption-Based Admissible Argumentation," Artificial Intelligence.

18. Eliot, Lance (2020). AI And Legal Reasoning Essentials. LBE Press Publishing.

19. Eliot, Lance (2020). Artificial Intelligence and LegalTech Essentials. LBE Press Publishing.

20. Eliot, Lance (2020). Decisive Essays on AI and Law. LBE Press Publishing.

21. Eliot, Lance (2020). Incisive Research on AI and Law. LBE Press Publishing.

22. Eliot, Lance (2020). "FutureLaw 2020 Showcases How Tech is Transforming The Law, Including the Impacts of AI," April 16, 2020, Forbes.

23. Erdem, Esra, and Michael Gelfond, Nicola Leone (2016). "Applications of Answer Set Programming," AI Magazine.

24. Gardner, Anne (1987). Artificial Intelligence and Legal Reasoning. MIT Press.

25. Genesereth, Michael (2009). "Computational Law: The Cop in the Backseat," Stanford Center for Legal Informatics, Stanford University.

26. Ghosh, Mirna (2019). "Automation of Legal Reasoning and Decision Based on Ontologies," Normandie Universite.

27. Grabmair, Matthias (2017). "Predicting Trade Secret Case Outcomes using Argument Schemes and Learned Quantitative Value Effect Tradeoffs," IJCAI June 12, 2017, London, United Kingdom.

28. Hage, Jaap (1996). "A Theory of Legal Reasoning and a Logic to Match," Volume 4, Artificial Intelligence and Law.

29. Hage, Jaap (2000). "Dialectical Models in Artificial Intelligence and Law," Artificial Intelligence and Law.

30. Hage, Japp, and Ronald Leenes, Arno Lodder (1993). "Hard Cases: A Procedural Approach," Artificial Intelligence and Law.

31. Hobbes, Thomas (1651). The Matter, Form, and Power of a Common-Wealth Ecclesiasticall and Civil.

32. Holmes, Oliver (1897). "The Path of the Law," Volume 10, Harvard Law Review.

33. Katz, Daniel, and Michael Bommarito, Josh Blackman (2017). "A General Approach for Predicting the Behavior of the Supreme Court of the United States," April 12, 2017, PLOS ONE.

34. Kowalski, Robert, and Francesca Toni (1996). "Abstract Argumentation," AI-Law96.

35. Laswell, Harold (1955). "Current Studies of the Decision Process: Automation Creativity," Volume 8, Western Political Quarterly.

36. Libal, Tomer, and Alexander Steen (2019). "The NAI Suite: Drafting and Reasoning over Legal Texts," October 15, 2019, arXiv.

37. Lipton, Zachary (2017). "The Mythos of Model Interpretability," March 6, 2017, arXiv.

38. Martin, Andrew, and Kevin Quinn, Theodore Ruger, Pauline Kim (2004). "Competing Approaches to Predicting Supreme Court Decision Making," December 2014, Symposium on Forecasting U.S. Supreme Court Decisions.

39. McCarty, Thorne (1977). "Reflections on TAXMAN: An Experiment in Artificial Intelligence and Legal Reasoning," January 1977, Harvard Law Review.

40. Modgil, Sanjay, and Henry Prakken (2013). "The ASPIC+ Framework for Structured Argumentation: A Tutorial," December 16, 2013, Argument & Computation.

41. Mowbray, Andrew, and Philip Chung, Graham Greenleaf (2019). "Utilising AI in the Legal Assistance Sector," LegalAIIA Workshop, ICAIL, June 17, 2019, Montreal, Canada.

42. Parasuraman, Raja, and Thomas Sheridan, Christopher Wickens (2000). "A Model for Types and Levels of Human Interaction with Automation," May 2000, IEEE Transactions on Systems, Man, and Cybernetics.

43. Popple, James (1993). "SHYSTER: A Pragmatic Legal Expert System," Ph.D. Dissertation, Australian National University.

44. Prakken, Henry, and Giovanni Sartor (2015). "Law and Logic: A Review from an Argumentation Perspective," Volume 227, Artificial Intelligence.

45. Rissland, Edwina (1988). Artificial Intelligence and Legal Reasoning: A Discussion of the Field and Gardner's Book," Volume 9, AI Magazine.

46. Rissland, Edwina (1990). "Artificial Intelligence and Law: Stepping Stones to a Model of Legal Reasoning," Yale Law Journal.

47. Searle, John (1980). "Minds, Brains, and Programs," Volume 3, Behavioral and Brain Sciences.

48. Sunstein, Cass (2001). "Of Artificial Intelligence and Legal Reasoning," University of Chicago Law School, Public Law and Legal Theory Working Papers.

49. Sunstein, Cass, and Kevin Ashley, Karl Branting, Howard Margolis (2001). "Legal Reasoning and Artificial Intelligence: How Computers 'Think' Like Lawyers," Symposium: Legal Reasoning and Artificial Intelligence, University of Chicago Law School Roundtable.

50. Surden, Harry (2014). "Machine Learning and Law," Washington Law Review.

51. Surden, Harry (2019). "Artificial Intelligence and Law: An Overview," Summer 2019, Georgia State University Law Review.

52. Valente, Andre, and Joost Breuker (1996). "A Functional Ontology of Law," Artificial Intelligence and Law.

53. Waltl, Bernhard, and Roland Vogl (2018). "Explainable Artificial Intelligence: The New Frontier in Legal Informatics," February 2018, Jusletter IT 22, Stanford Center for Legal Informatics, Stanford University.

54. Wittgenstein, Ludwig (1953). Philosophical Investigations. Blackwell Publishing.

APPENDIX B
SUPPLEMENTAL
FIGURES AND CHARTS

For the convenience of viewing, supplemental figures and charts related to the topics discussed are shown on the next pages

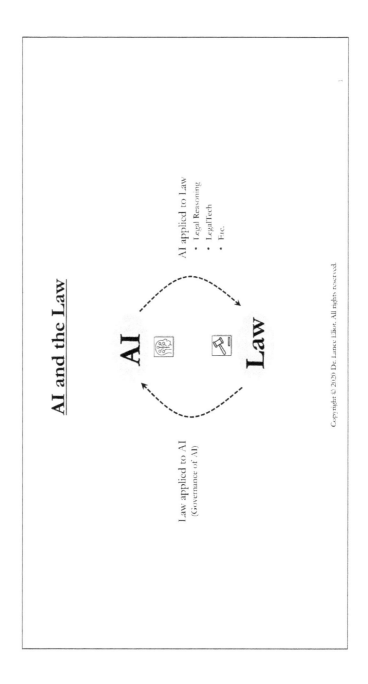

Figure 1

AI & Law: Levels of Autonomy For AI Legal Reasoning (AILR)

v1.3

Level	Descriptor	Examples	Automation	Status
0	No Automation	Manual, paper-based (no automation)	None	De Facto - In Use
1	Simple Assistance Automation	Word Processing, XLS, online legal docs, etc.	Legal Assist	Widely In Use
2	Advanced Assistance Automation	Query-style NLP, ML for case prediction, etc.	Legal Assist	Some In Use
3	Semi-Autonomous Automation	KBS & ML/DL for legal reasoning & analysis, etc.	Legal Assist	Primarily Prototypes & Research Based
4	AILR Domain Autonomous	Versed only in a specific legal domain	Legal Advisor (law fluent)	None As Yet
5	AILR Fully Autonomous	Versatile within and across all legal domains	Legal Advisor (law fluent)	None As Yet
6	AILR Superhuman Autonomous	Exceeds human-based legal reasoning	Supra Legal Advisor	Indeterminate

Source Author: Dr. Lance B. Eliot

Figure 1: AI & Law - Autonomous Levels by Rows

Figure 2

AI & Law: Levels of Autonomy For AI Legal Reasoning (AILR)

	Level 0	Level 1	Level 2	Level 3	Level 4	Level 5	Level 6
Descriptor	No Automation	Simple Assistance Automation	Advanced Assistance Automation	Semi-Autonomous Automation	AILR Domain Autonomous	AILR Fully Autonomous	AILR Superhuman Autonomous
Examples	Manual, paper-based (no automation)	Word Processing, XLS, online legal docs, etc.	Query-style NLP, ML for case prediction, etc.	KBS & ML/DL for legal reasoning & analysis, etc.	Versed only in a specific legal domain	Versatile within and across all legal domains	Exceeds human-based legal reasoning
Automation	None	Legal Assist	Legal Assist	Legal Assist	Legal Advisor (law fluent)	Legal Advisor (law fluent)	Supra Legal Advisor
Status	De Facto – In Use	Widely In Use	Some In Use	Primarily Prototypes & Research-based	None As Yet	None As Yet	Indeterminate

Figure 2: AI & Law - Autonomous Levels by Columns

Source Author: Dr. Lance B. Eliot

v1.3

Figure 3

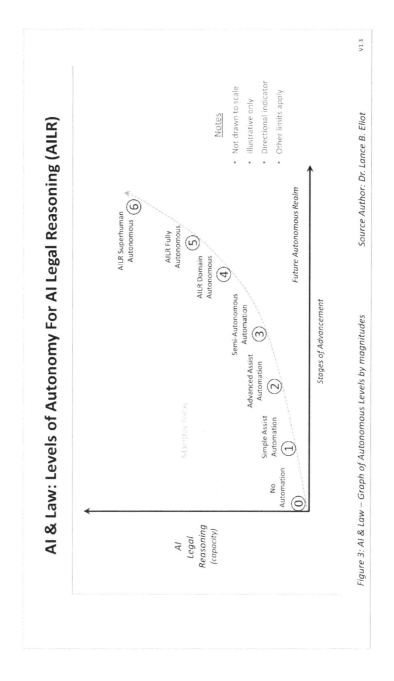

Figure 3: AI & Law – Graph of Autonomous Levels by magnitudes

Figure 4

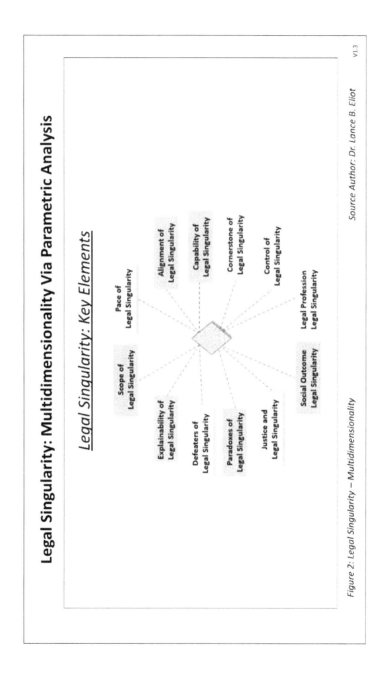

Figure 2: Legal Singularity – Multidimensionality

Figure 5

196

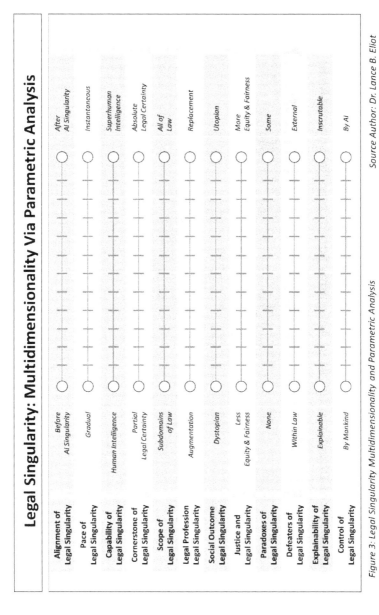

Figure 3: Legal Singularity Multidimensionality and Parametric Analysis

Figure 6

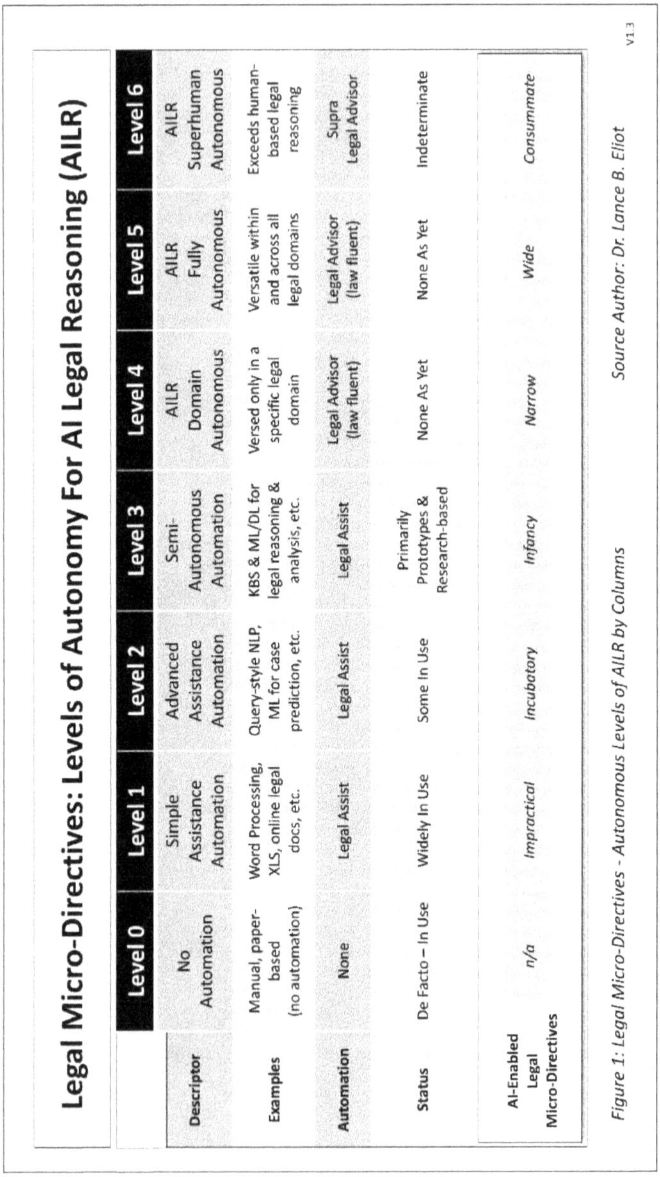

Legal Micro-Directives: Levels of Autonomy For AI Legal Reasoning (AILR)

Descriptor	Level 0	Level 1	Level 2	Level 3	Level 4	Level 5	Level 6
Descriptor	No Automation	Simple Assistance Automation	Advanced Assistance Automation	Semi-Autonomous Automation	AILR Domain Autonomous	AILR Fully Autonomous	AILR Superhuman Autonomous
Examples	Manual, paper-based (no automation)	Word Processing, XLS, online legal docs, etc.	Query-style NLP, ML for case prediction, etc.	KBS & ML/DL for legal reasoning & analysis, etc.	Versed only in a specific legal domain	Versatile within and across all legal domains	Exceeds human-based legal reasoning
Automation	None	Legal Assist	Legal Assist	Legal Assist	Legal Advisor (law fluent)	Legal Advisor (law fluent)	Supra Legal Advisor
Status	De Facto – In Use	Widely In Use	Some In Use	Primarily Prototypes & Research-based	None As Yet	None As Yet	Indeterminate
AI-Enabled Legal Micro-Directives	n/a	Impractical	Incubatory	Infancy	Narrow	Wide	Consummate

v1.3

Figure 1: Legal Micro-Directives - Autonomous Levels of AILR by Columns   *Source Author: Dr. Lance B. Eliot*

Figure 7

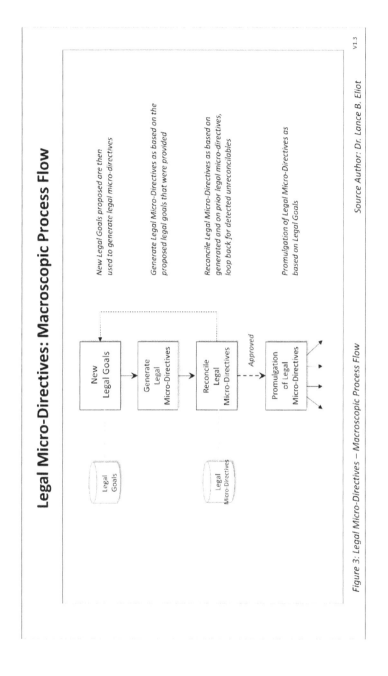

Legal Micro-Directives: Macroscopic Process Flow

New Legal Goals proposed are then used to generate legal micro-directives

Generate Legal Micro-Directives as based on the proposed legal goals that were provided

Reconcile Legal Micro-Directives as based on generated and on prior legal micro-directives, loop back for detected unreconcilables

Promulgation of Legal Micro-Directives as based on Legal Goals

New Legal Goals

Generate Legal Micro-Directives

Reconcile Legal Micro-Directives

Approved

Promulgation of Legal Micro-Directives

Legal Goals

Legal Micro-Directives

Source Author: Dr. Lance B. Eliot

V1.3

Figure 3: Legal Micro-Directives – Macroscopic Process Flow

Figure 8

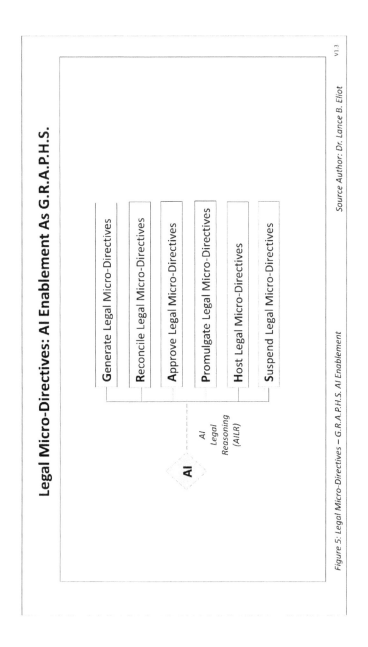

Figure 9

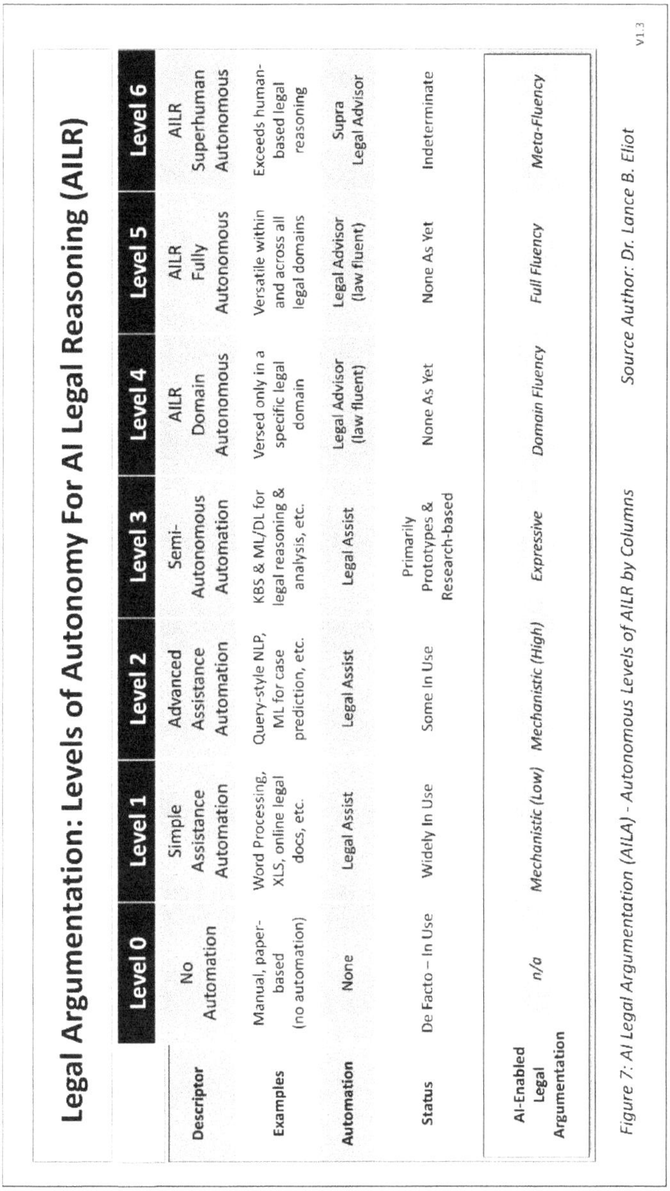

Legal Argumentation: Levels of Autonomy For AI Legal Reasoning (AILR)

	Level 0	Level 1	Level 2	Level 3	Level 4	Level 5	Level 6
Descriptor	No Automation	Simple Assistance Automation	Advanced Assistance Automation	Semi-Autonomous Automation	AILR Domain Autonomous	AILR Fully Autonomous	AILR Superhuman Autonomous
Examples	Manual, paper-based (no automation)	Word Processing, XLS, online legal docs, etc.	Query-style NLP, ML for case prediction, etc.	KBS & ML/DL for legal reasoning & analysis, etc.	Versed only in a specific legal domain	Versatile within and across all legal domains	Exceeds human-based legal reasoning
Automation	None	Legal Assist	Legal Assist	Legal Assist	Legal Advisor (law fluent)	Legal Advisor (law fluent)	Supra Legal Advisor
Status	De Facto – In Use	Widely In Use	Some In Use	Primarily Prototypes & Research-based	None As Yet	None As Yet	Indeterminate
AI-Enabled Legal Argumentation	n/a	Mechanistic (Low)	Mechanistic (High)	Expressive	Domain Fluency	Full Fluency	Meta-Fluency

Figure 7: AI Legal Argumentation (AILA) - Autonomous Levels of AILR by Columns   *Source Author: Dr. Lance B. Eliot*

v1.3

Figure 10

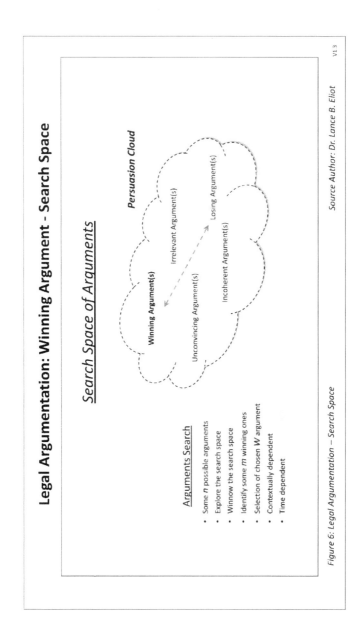

Figure 11

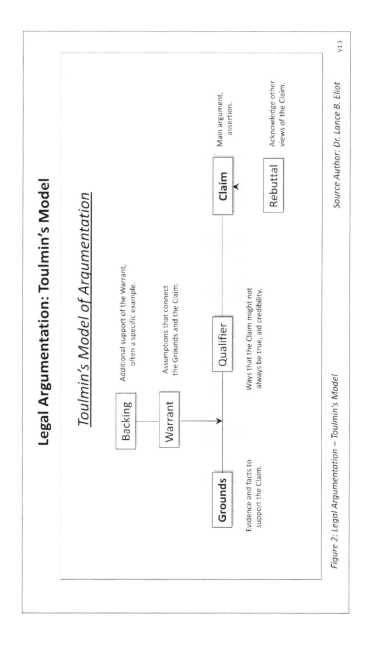

Figure 2: Legal Argumentation – Toulmin's Model

Figure 12

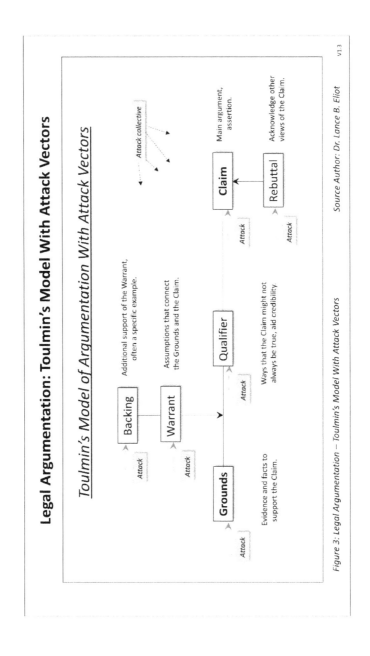

Figure 13

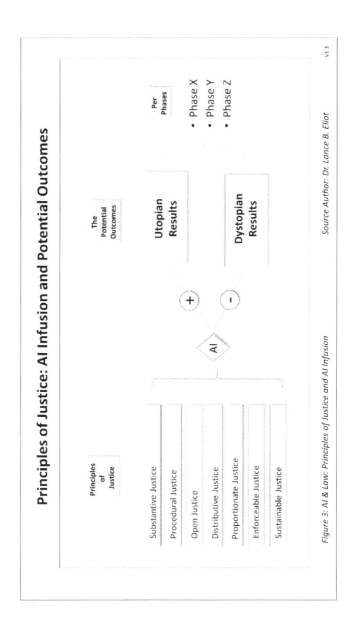

Figure 14

Principles of Justice and Autonomous Levels of AI Legal Reasoning (AILR)

Descriptor	Level 0 No Automation	Level 1 Simple Assistance Automation	Level 2 Advanced Assistance Automation	Level 3 Semi-Autonomous Automation	Level 4 AILR Domain Autonomous	Level 5 AILR Fully Autonomous	Level 6 AILR Superhuman Autonomous
Substantive Justice	Traditional	Traditional	Traditional	Emerging	Phase X Impacts	Phase Y Impacts	Phase Z Impacts
Procedural Justice	Traditional	Traditional	Traditional	Emerging	Phase X Impacts	Phase Y Impacts	Phase Z Impacts
Open Justice	Traditional	Traditional	Traditional	Emerging	Phase X Impacts	Phase Y Impacts	Phase Z Impacts
Distributive Justice	Traditional	Traditional	Traditional	Emerging	Phase X Impacts	Phase Y Impacts	Phase Z Impacts
Proportionate Justice	Traditional	Traditional	Traditional	Emerging	Phase X Impacts	Phase Y Impacts	Phase Z Impacts
Enforceable Justice	Traditional	Traditional	Traditional	Emerging	Phase X Impacts	Phase Y Impacts	Phase Z Impacts
Sustainable Justice	Traditional	Traditional	Traditional	Emerging	Phase X Impacts	Phase Y Impacts	Phase Z Impacts

v1.3

Figure 1: AI & Law – Principles of Justice and LoA AILR by Columns

Source Author: Dr. Lance B. Eliot

Figure 15

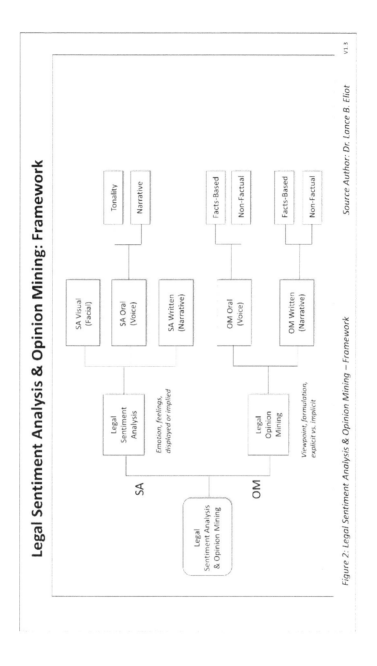

Figure 16

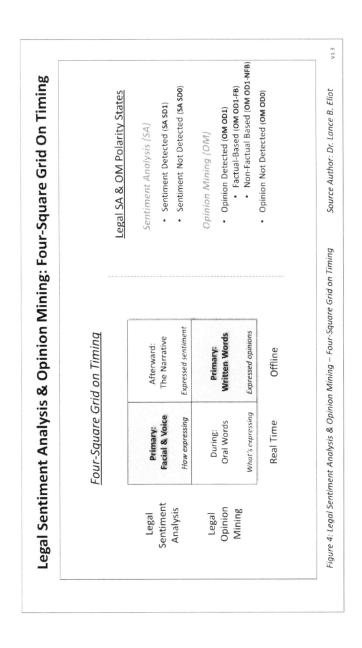

Figure 4: Legal Sentiment Analysis & Opinion Mining – Four-Square Grid on Timing

Figure 17

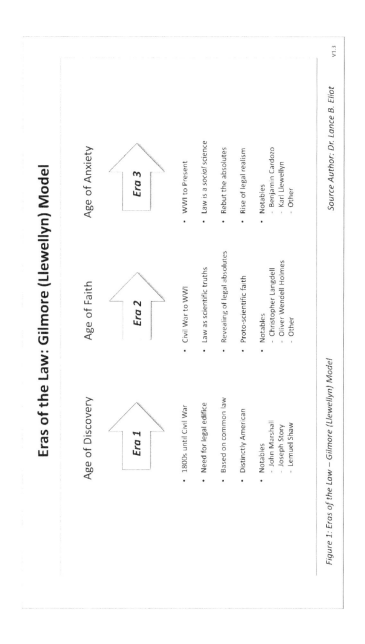

Figure 1: Eras of the Law – Gilmore (Llewellyn) Model

Figure 18

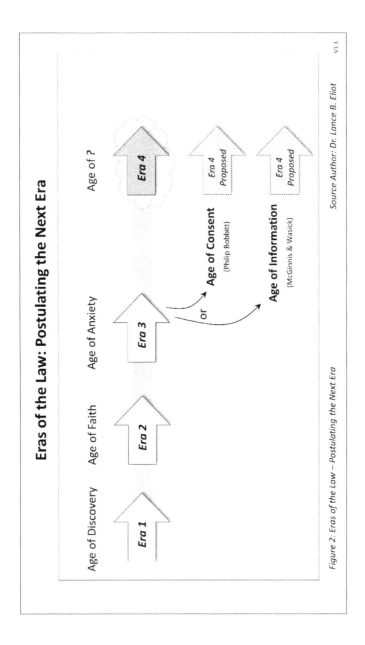

Figure 19

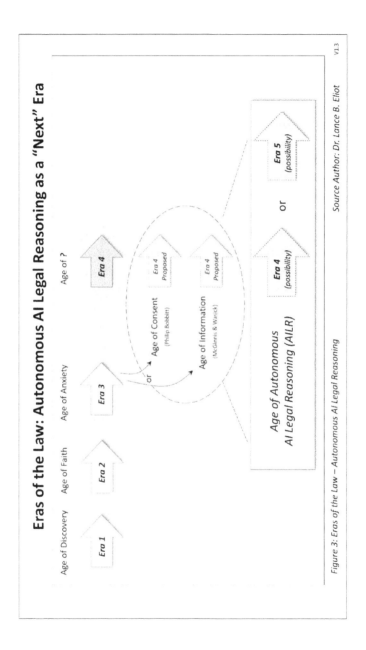

Figure 20

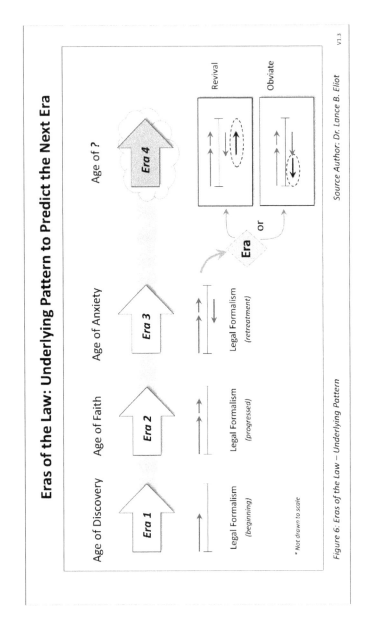

Figure 21

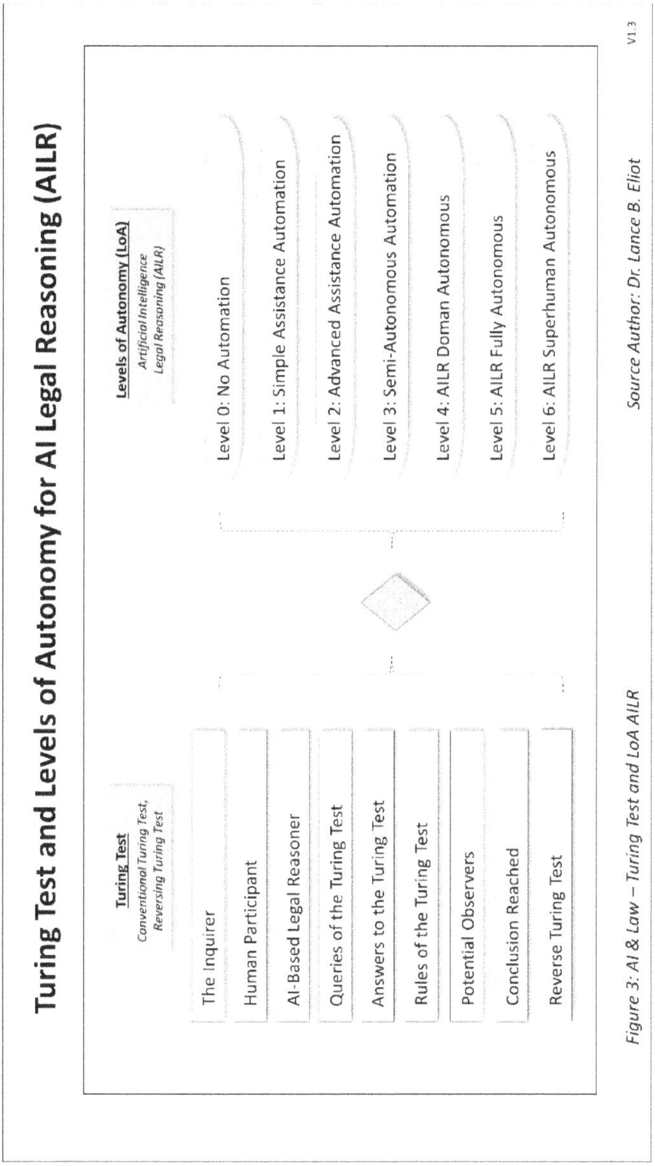
Turing Test and Levels of Autonomy for AI Legal Reasoning (AILR)
Turing Test
Conventional Turing Test,
Reversing Turing Test
The Inquirer
Human Participant
AI-Based Legal Reasoner
Queries of the Turing Test
Answers to the Turing Test
Rules of the Turing Test
Potential Observers
Conclusion Reached
Reverse Turing Test
Levels of Autonomy (LoA)
Artificial Intelligence
Legal Reasoning (AILR)
Level 0: No Automation
Level 1: Simple Assistance Automation
Level 2: Advanced Assistance Automation
Level 3: Semi-Autonomous Automation
Level 4: AILR Doman Autonomous
Level 5: AILR Fully Autonomous
Level 6: AILR Superhuman Autonomous
Figure 3: AI & Law – Turing Test and LoA AILR
Source Author: Dr. Lance B. Eliot
V1.3

Figure 22

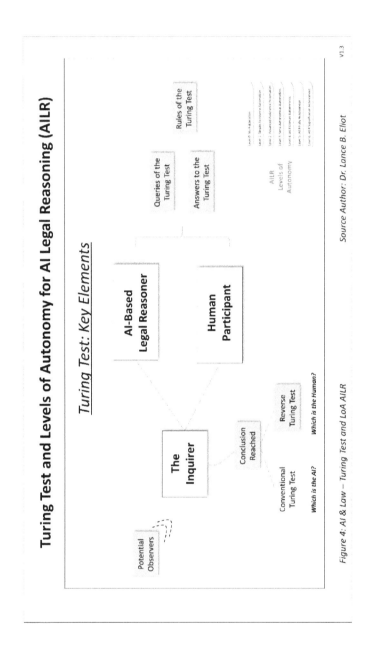

Figure 23

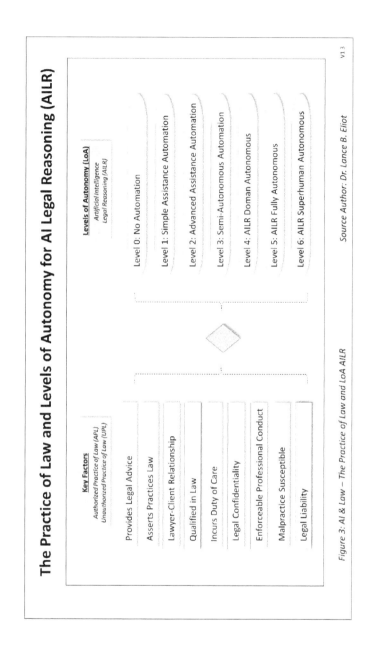

Figure 24

The Practice of Law and Autonomous Levels of AI Legal Reasoning (AILR)

V1.3

Strawman Variant

Descriptor	Level 0 No Automation	Level 1 Simple Assistance Automation	Level 2 Advanced Assistance Automation	Level 3 Semi-Autonomous Automation	Level 4 AILR Domain Autonomous	Level 5 AILR Fully Autonomous	Level 6 AILR Superhuman Autonomous
Provides Legal Advice	n/a	No	Maybe	Yes	Yes	Yes	Yes Plus
Asserts Practices Law	n/a	No	No	No	Yes	Yes	Yes Plus
Lawyer-Client Relationship	n/a	No	No	No	Partial	Yes	Yes
Qualified in Law	n/a	No	No	Minimal	Partial	Yes	Yes Plus
Incurs Duty of Care	n/a	No	No	No	Likely	Yes	Yes
Legal Confidentiality	n/a	No	No	No	Likely	Yes	Yes
Enforceable Prof Conduct	n/a	No	No	No	Likely	Yes	Yes
Malpractice Susceptible	n/a	No	No	No	Likely	Yes	Yes
Legal Liability	n/a	No	Maybe	Likely	Likely	Yes	Yes

Source Author: Dr. Lance B. Eliot

Figure 1: AI & Law – The Practice of Law and LoA AILR by Columns

Figure 25

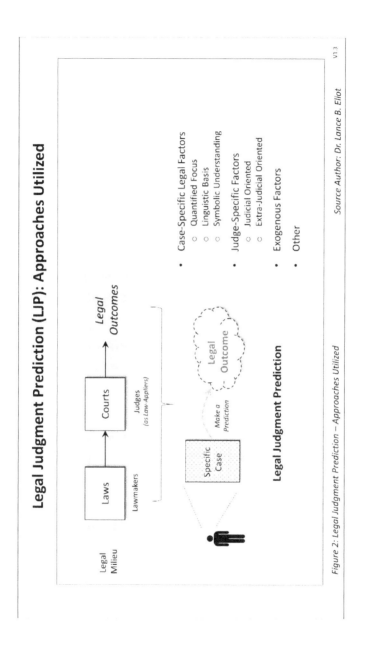

Figure 26

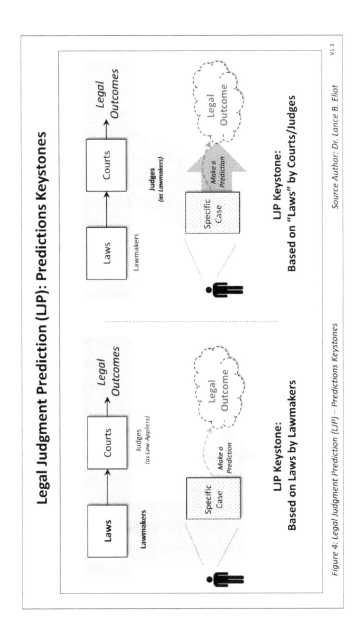

Figure 27

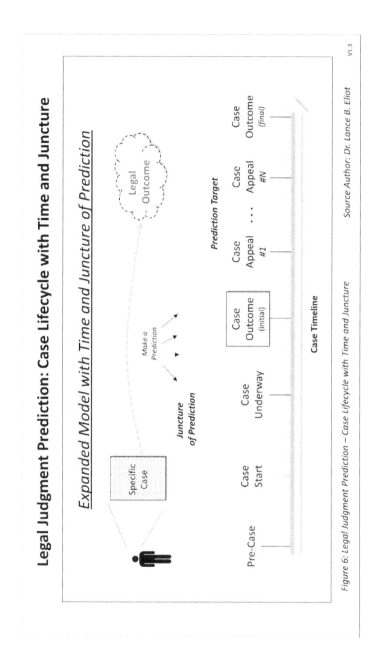

Figure 28

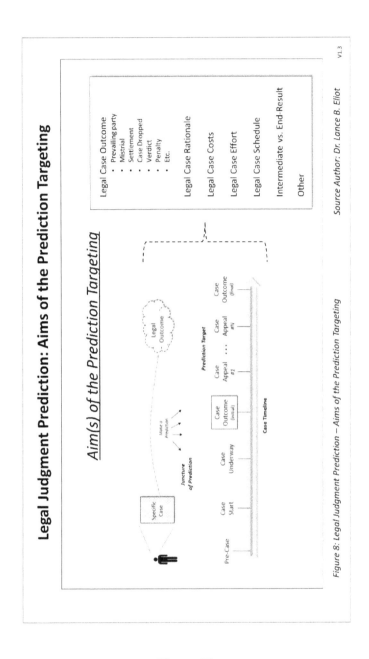

Figure 8: Legal Judgment Prediction – Aims of the Prediction Targeting

Figure 29

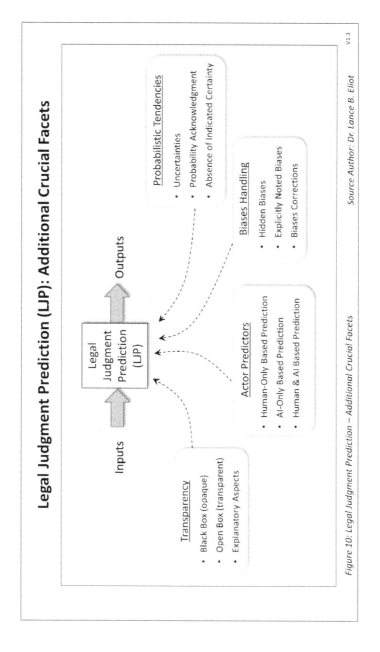

Figure 10: Legal Judgment Prediction – Additional Crucial Facets

Figure 30

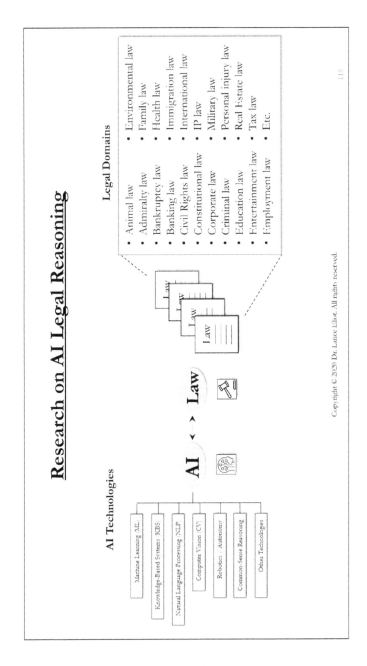

Figure 31

ABOUT THE AUTHOR

Dr. Lance B. Eliot, Ph.D., MBA is a globally recognized AI expert and thought leader, an invited Stanford Fellow at Stanford University, an experienced top executive and corporate leader, a successful entrepreneur, and a noted scholar on AI, including that his Forbes and AI Trends columns have amassed over 4 million views, his books on AI are ranked in the Top 10 of all-time AI books, his journal articles are widely cited, and he has developed and implemented numerous AI systems.

He currently serves as the Chief AI Scientist at Techbruim, Inc. and has over twenty years of industry experience including serving as a corporate officer in billion-dollar sized firms and was a partner in a major consulting firm. He is also a successful entrepreneur having founded, ran, and sold several high-tech related businesses.

Dr. Eliot previously hosted the popular radio show *Technotrends* that was also available on American Airlines flights via their in-flight audio program, he has made appearances on CNN, has been a frequent speaker at industry conferences, and his podcasts have been downloaded over 150,000 times.

A former professor at the University of Southern California (USC), he founded and led an innovative research lab on Artificial Intelligence. He also previously served on the faculty of the University of California Los Angeles (UCLA) and was a visiting professor at other major universities. He was elected to the International Board of the Society for Information Management (SIM), a prestigious association of over 3,000 high-tech executives worldwide.

He has performed extensive community service, including serving as Senior Science Adviser to the Congressional Vice-Chair of the Congressional Committee on Science & Technology. He has served on the Board of the OC Science & Engineering Fair (OCSEF), where he is also has been a Grand Sweepstakes judge, and likewise served as a judge for the Intel International SEF (ISEF). He served as the Vice-Chair of the Association for Computing Machinery (ACM) Chapter, a prestigious association of computer scientists. Dr. Eliot has been a shark tank judge for the USC Mark Stevens Center for Innovation on start-up pitch competitions and served as a mentor for several incubators and accelerators in Silicon Valley and in Silicon Beach.

Dr. Eliot holds a Ph.D. from USC, MBA, and Bachelor's in Computer Science, and earned the CDP, CCP, CSP, CDE, and CISA certifications

ADDENDUM

Thanks for reading this book and I hope you will continue your interest in the field of AI & Law

----

For my free podcasts about AI & Law:

https://ai-law.libsyn.com/website

Those podcasts are also available on Spotify, iTunes, etc.

For the latest on AI & Law see my website:

www.ai-law.legal

To follow me on Twitter:

https://twitter.com/LanceEliot

For my in-depth book on AI & Law:

AI And Legal Reasoning Essentials

www.amazon.com/gp/product/1734601655/

www.ingramcontent.com/pod-product-compliance
Lightning Source LLC
Chambersburg PA
CBHW071111050326
40690CB00008B/1191